Illuminating
the Way

"Christine Valters Paintner creates a vibrant green path—a path I love to walk. In *Illuminating the Way*, she invites saints and mystics to join us on that path. The Hebrew prophet Miriam, the Celtic monk Brendan, and contemporary writers like Rainer Maria Rilke and Thomas Merton—along with eight others—step out of their books, walk beside us, and do, indeed, illumine the path."

Janet Conner
Author of *Writing Down Your Soul*

"In this creative work, Christine Valters Paintner offers us a pilgrimage through the lives of sages, healers, mystics, visionaries, and more—inviting us to feast on their wisdom and explore how their gift of life can illuminate the way for us. This is a wonderful resource and I joyfully recommend it."

Macrina Wiederkehr, O.S.B.
Author of *Seven Sacred Pauses*

"*Illuminating the Way* combines meditation, poetry, art, and more to reveal the singing heart of our tradition's great wisdom keepers. Jesus has been called the Lord of the Dance—this sumptuous book calls us to join the circle."

Carl McColman
Author of *Befriending Silence*

"*Illuminating the Way* generously offers myriad pathways to discover and explore the multiple selves that dwell within each of us. It's a book that will expand you, a real treasure that you will return to again and again."

Colette Lafia
Author of *Seeking Surrender*

Illuminating the Way

EMBRACING THE WISDOM OF MONKS AND MYSTICS

Christine Valters Paintner

Icons by Marcy Hall

With Biblical Reflections by John Valters Paintner

SORIN BOOKS Notre Dame, Indiana

Scripture quotations are from the *New Revised Standard Version* of the Bible, copyright © 1993 and 1989 by the Division of Christian Education of the National Council of Churches of Christ in the USA. Used by permission. All rights reserved.

The appendix, "How to Practice Lectio Divina," is reprinted from *Lectio Divina—The Sacred Art*, copyright ©2011, Christine Valters Paintner. Used by permission of SkyLight Paths Publishing.

Icons used by permission of Marcy Hall. All rights reserved.

Mandala illustrations used by permission of Stacy Wills. All rights reserved.

----

www.sorinbooks.com

Paperback: ISBN-13 978-1-933495-93-4

E-book: ISBN-13 978-1-933495-94-1

Cover images © Marcy Hall.

Cover and text design by Katherine J. Ross.

Printed and bound in the United States of America.

Library of Congress Cataloging-in-Publication Data
Names: Paintner, Christine Valters, author.
Title: Illuminating the way : embracing the wisdom of monks and mystics /
    Christine Valters Paintner ; icons by Marcy Hall ; with biblical
    reflections by John Valters Paintner.
Description: Notre Dame : Sorin Books, 2016. | Includes bibliographical
    references.
Identifiers: LCCN 2015047356 (print) | LCCN 2016005626 (ebook) | ISBN
    9781933495934 (pbk.) | ISBN 9781933495941 (e-book)
Subjects: LCSH: Spiritual life--Christianity.
Classification: LCC BV4501.3 .P3358 2016 (print) | LCC BV4501.3 (ebook) | DDC
    248.4--dc23
LC record available at http://lccn.loc.gov/2015047356

With deep gratitude for the witness of monks and mystics through the ages,
offering new and ancient wisdom to help illuminate the way ahead.
This book is dedicated to all of the dancing monks who
strive to keep this wisdom alive.

Contents

Acknowledgments

. . . .

The creative process of writing a book is pure joy for me, and even more so in this particular work where I had the opportunity and gift to immerse myself in the wisdom of these incredible figures from our past. I am grateful for their witness to a life of soulfulness and commitment and to the One who animated their service with such love.

I offer great gratitude to artist Marcy Hall who offered such an enthusiastic yes when I suggested this project to her of painting the "dancing monk" icons. I love the way she brought these figures to life through color, playfulness, and joy. Gratitude also goes to artist Stacy Wills who generously supplied the mandala coloring pages for this book.

I am very grateful to my dear friend and teaching partner Betsey Beckman who suggested that we ask various musician friends of ours to create songs to accompany each monk and mystic, and then she offered to choreograph dance prayers for each song. She has created a CD *Singing with Monks and Mystics* and a DVD *Dancing with Monks and Mystics* that can be ordered at my website, AbbeyoftheArts.com.

Thanks goes to my amazing spiritual community, the Holy Disorder of Dancing Monks, at Abbey of the Arts and especially to those who participated in the online retreats for Advent 2014 and New Year's 2015 and were the first to engage with this material in such whole-hearted ways that their enthusiasm spurred me on.

I am always grateful for my ongoing relationship with Sorin Books, especially Bob Hamma, who is always such a wonderful supporter of my work and helped to edit this book. The whole team is great to work with.

Last, but definitely not least, is a deep bow of gratitude to my beloved husband, John Valters Paintner, who contributed the scripture reflections, his area of passion and expertise, for his ongoing love and support for me. As I finish these edits we are nearing our twenty-first wedding anniversary, and as our vocations deepen and intertwine, life together just seems to get more and more magical.

Introduction

· ·

This book takes you on a journey accompanied by many great monks and mystics of our tradition. While there are other worthy books that invite you into relationship with the saints, what makes this one unique is that each figure invites us into an exploration of a particular archetypal energy within us. In my work with others, I have found this an especially helpful approach. Suddenly a particular figure from our sacred tradition becomes even more relevant to our lives because they help us to illuminate parts of ourselves that need further development to grow in wholeness and in our relationship to God.

EXPLAINING THE ARCHETYPES
Carl Jung believed there were two levels to our unconscious. The first was the personal level created by personal experience, and the second was the collective level consisting of instinctual and universal patterns of thought developed in human beings over thousands of years. These primordial blueprints are called archetypes and form the foundation of our experience.

We each have within us a gathering of different energies. Archetypes appear across cultures and traditions, in myths, stories, and dreams. By exploring a particular archetype we can reflect on how it is alive in us, how we have suppressed this aspect, and how it might illumine our own personal shadows and areas of growth. They can help us move toward our own growing wholeness and freedom.

We find archetypes active in our nighttime dreams. They are active within each of us as a multiplicity of energies that we can draw upon. When we are living from a place of balance and fullness we have access to more dimensions of ourselves.

Most of us tend to identify with a few dominant archetypes. Maybe you find a powerful sense of life purpose in caring for others and identify more with the Mother archetype. Maybe your story carries a lot of abandonment and you identify with the Orphan. In my work at Abbey of the Arts and in my book *The Artist's Rule: Nurturing Your Creative Soul with Monastic Wisdom*, I primarily explore the inner Monk (the aspect of us seeking presence to the sacred in all things) and inner Artist (the aspect of us seeking to give form and expression to beauty in the world).

Jung described the four main universal archetypes as the Self, the Shadow, the Animus and Anima, and the Persona. I will briefly explore the first two and encourage you to see the resource section at the end of this book for further information on the others.

DEFINING THE SELF, SHADOW, AND PROJECTION

The Self is that internal, unifying aspect of ourselves, bringing together conscious and unconscious. When we live from the Self we live from our place of deepest authenticity and truth with access to a full range of inner energies. Jung described the journey toward this kind of truthfulness and integration as individuation.

The unconscious contains what Jung called "shadow" material. This shadow contains all the things about ourselves that have become repressed and we are too ashamed of to allow into the light. We also have what he called a "golden shadow," which are all of the positive qualities about ourselves we don't allow out.

Projection is the act of seeing our own shadow material in someone else's behavior, so we get activated in response. Consider people in your life who really annoy you and get under your skin. These people are mirroring back to you a part of yourself that has been disowned and needs to be integrated again.

We also project our golden shadow on others, which is revealed by those people we idolize and put up on pedestals. They are mirroring an aspect of yourself that you are afraid to claim.

WELCOMING YOUR MULTITUDE

My husband John and I pray lectio divina most mornings together. We also pray what is known as *lectio continua,* or the ancient practice of choosing a book of the scriptures and then praying through a couple of verses each day until we reach the end. It is a version of monastic stability, of staying with something through all of its ups and downs. It causes us to pray texts we might otherwise avoid. Recently we worked through the Song of Songs in this way, and now we are praying the psalms one by one.

One morning we found ourselves in the midst of Psalm 10, a difficult psalm of lament. Instead of reading all the way through to the end and finding immediate resolution in the psalmist's cry of hope to God, we sat each day with two verses at a time, with haunting questions about God's presence echoing through. It was disturbing to dwell on the images of the "enemies," the ones whose "mouths are filled with cursing and deceit and oppression," or those who "murder the innocent" and "stealthily watch for the helpless." The psalmist later calls out to God to "break the arm of the wicked." As I sat with these images I wanted to turn away and say these have nothing to do with me and my peaceful life.

Yet, in prayer the invitation arose: What are the ways I deceive myself? What are the places of opposition within my own heart? How do I "murder" my own innocence? How do I take advantage of that which feels helpless within? How do I fuel my own self-destruction?

I discovered the psalms as a beautiful gateway of awareness into my own inner multitude.

Our heads and hearts are full of crazy, often self-defeating, competing voices. We are each a multitude of differing energies and personalities. We contain within us the parts that feel tender and ashamed alongside the courageous and fierce, the joyful and giddy. It often feels easier to simply push the voices away, but it is exhausting.

A lot of our inner conflict comes from our stubborn refusal to make space for the multiplicity we contain. One of my favorite lines from the *Rule* of Benedict, that sixth-century source of great wisdom for daily living, is "all guests who present themselves are to be welcomed as Christ, for he himself will say: I was a stranger and you welcomed me." I love this invitation to welcome that which feels the most strange as the very face of God. The door might be outside of us, but just as easily it is within. We each have parts of ourselves we try to push away.

These voices often fight within us for primacy. They each want to define who we are. Especially loud can be the inner Judge, who thinks she knows everything. She sounds very authoritative.

There is a deeper and wiser voice, which is the Self, sometimes called the inner Witness. It is the calm and compassionate part that can sit in the center of all this chaos and behold it. It is the part we develop through meditation, and it is not carried away by conflicting inner demands. This is the voice of the soul. In our archetypal work, Christ could be considered the exemplar of this presence within us.

When we continue to follow the Judge or the inner Critic or any of the especially loud and forceful voices inside of us without recourse to the whole range of who we are, we often find ourselves full of self-doubt and insecurity, and we become depleted.

These voices often originated as a way of protecting ourselves. The Judge can help us to discern what is true and good. The Critic can help cut away the excess.

Not all of the voices within us are "negative." Many of these energies can offer us tremendous resources for living in an empowered way. Some of my favorites are the inner Warrior, who helps me to set healthy boundaries. My inner Orphan reminds me that I have a lot of tenderness within, which just wants to be witnessed and not fixed. My inner Lover calls me to follow my passions in life, to remember that what I am in love with—whether ideas or communities or people—will ignite vitality in my work.

Each archetype has a shadow side and a light side. Exploring them illuminates our places of growth, helps break old patterns, calls us to step fully into our deepest passions in service to the world, and ultimately bring us to a place of greater internal freedom. They can be deeply supportive of the creative process, opening up access to different resources within us. The archetypes can offer us a powerful support for our creative living and reflection on what our passions are and what holds us back. They connect us to the place where the Spirit is alive and moving in us. The archetypes, in their fullness, are also different names for and dimensions of the divine.

When we over-identify with one or two archetypes our lives feel more narrow and constricting. When we suppress energies that want to be lived out in our lives we experience a gnawing sense of dissatisfaction. We sense there is a greater fullness awaiting us, but we need to draw on different energies to access this inner spaciousness—for some the Warrior is a challenging energy to experience, and yet it is the place within us that creates strong boundaries and protection for what is most valuable. For others, the Sovereign may be a place of growth; calling upon this archetype can offer a sense of strength in taking full responsibility for your choices in life.

A shadow overeager Warrior can become destructive or set boundaries that don't let anyone in. An Orphan who feels completely abandoned can continue the cycle by cutting off relationships out of fear of being hurt. And the Lover who is out of balance may find him- or herself envious of the others who follow what lights them on fire.

The Self or Witness within us always speaks with tremendous compassion, always invites us to begin again. This voice can behold and welcome in all of the parts who want to speak and not be overwhelmed by the demands of a single one. The Self can see where the shadowed and hurting places are and respond with gentleness and kindness, and yet it can also call in a powerful fierceness when needed.

This is the gift of working with the archetypes. Monastic wisdom tells us that hospitality is key. Welcome in the stranger, even if that stranger is me, or at least parts of me.

The psalms can become a mirror to the shadow places within you. But other verses can also call forth the beauty and longings of your heart. They can remind you of the grace found in boundaries, in tenderness, and in passion. You are a multitude. My deepest hope in this book is that it inspires you to welcome in all of the parts of you.

CONNECTING JESUS, THE ARCHETYPES, AND THE INNER WITNESS

Theologian Walter Wink offers an interpretation of the gospel story of the Ascension that focuses on it not as a historical event but as an imaginal act to be undergone.[1] It is about not the record of facts but the transformation of power. He describes the event of the Ascension as Jesus entering the archetypal realm. Jesus becomes one with the divine, entering into the fullness of his power and offering us a vision of what that power looks like for each of us. Ascension is in part about connecting to Source and living from that power so that we might contribute to changing the world. When we live from our own sense of power, we encourage others to do the same, simply by the way we act in the world.

Carl Jung wrote, "What happens in the life of Christ happens always and everywhere."[2] Each chapter of this book will also briefly explore Jesus as an expression of the archetype through a gospel story. In the book *The Christian Archetype: A Jungian Commentary on the Life of Christ*, Jungian analyst Edward F. Edinger describes the patterns of Jesus' life from Annunciation to Pentecost as a series of archetypal events that are mirrored in our human experience.

Jesus, as the embodiment of the divine in human flesh, mirrors the array of gifts we can claim within ourselves and is also a witness to our own capacity to touch the sacred spark within each of us. The way of Christ points to a path of living from this inner Witness.

AN OVERVIEW OF THE CHAPTERS

This book takes you on a journey accompanied by many great monks and mystics of our tradition. In the chapters that follow we will move through a large span of time, from the prophet Miriam of the Hebrew scriptures all the way to the twentieth-century monk Thomas Merton. In chapter 1, we meet Francis of Assisi, who calls out our inner Fool, that part of ourselves willing to look foolish for the sake of following a call and turns expectations upside down. Chapter 2 explores King David, from the Hebrew scriptures, calling forth our own inner Sovereign, that part of ourselves that is empowered to take full responsibility for our choices in life. We then encounter our inner Mother in chapter

3, through the guidance of Mary, that source of vast compassion and love in our lives. In chapter 4 we learn from Dorothy Day the power of tending to our inner Orphan, that tender aspect of ourselves that has been abandoned by the world.

Chapter 5 brings us to Amma Syncletica, one of the desert mothers, who calls forth our inner Warrior, that aspect of ourselves able to set clear boundaries and protect what is most essential. Chapter 6 offers an invitation to explore the Healer through Brigid of Kildare and to open up to our own capacity for coming to wholeness in our lives. Brendan the Navigator calls us to encounter our inner Pilgrim, the dimension that longs to journey, in chapter 7. In chapter 8 we meet our inner Sage, that source of wisdom within us, through the lens of Benedict of Nursia.

The figure of Miriam from the Hebrew scriptures, instrumental in the Exodus story, calls forth our own inner Prophet in chapter 9, that part of ourselves willing to stand up to the status quo. Next, chapter 10 breaks open our inner Artist through the guidance of the great poet Rainer Maria Rilke. In chapter 11, Hildegard of Bingen will invite us to consider our inner Visionary, that part of ourselves that is able to imagine new possibilities. And finally, chapter 12 brings us modern monk Thomas Merton, who invites us to consider our own inner Monk and that part of ourselves seeking the face of God through silence and solitude.

Each chapter offers a wealth of possibilities for reflection and follows a similar pattern, beginning with a contemporary icon and followed by a reflection on the particular monk or mystic under consideration. Then each chapter breaks open the energy of the archetype in both light and shadow forms and connects this archetype to a gospel story about Jesus with a reflection written by my husband, John Paintner. There is a suggested spiritual practice to work with this energy and a meditation to meet it within yourself. You are then invited into a visual art exploration through various mandala creation practices. The chapters each close with some questions for reflection, and a poem I have written, inspired by the particular monk or mystic, is offered as a closing blessing.

THE EXPRESSIVE ARTS

You will be invited in each chapter to explore the energy of a given archetype through creative practices such as mandalas and writing. My approach to such creative explorations is firmly grounded in the field of the expressive arts.

The expressive arts developed as a way to integrate the various art modalities and to honor each one as a unique language of the soul. Working with the arts in an interdisciplinary and connected way offers deeper insight than when used in isolation from each other. You will notice in the mandala exercises, I often suggest beginning with gentle movement to awaken energy and closing with a written exploration to name the experience. These are ways of allowing the arts to deepen an encounter.

The expressive arts arise out of an understanding that we each speak a variety of languages. In our everyday life we may be most conscious of our verbal, analytic, and linear ways of communicating, rooted in the left brain experience. However, we have multiple ways of knowing within our very being that include the intuitive, visual, poetic, kinesthetic, and musical.

The expressive arts enlarge our capacity to see the holy at work in the world. Through this process we reclaim an ancient tradition of allowing the arts to open us to the multiple ways in which the sacred speaks to us. The arts afford us insights into life and the movements of the Spirit in our lives that are not available through cognitive ways of knowing, and they present us alternative possibilities.

In the expressive arts, our body knowledge, intuitive wisdom, and emotions are expressed through symbol and shape, poetry and color, movement and music, and are honored as valid ways of knowing in and of themselves. Rational analysis is not required to validate the insights gained. Artistic knowing is different from intellectual knowing, engaging us symbolically and in embodied ways, stretching us beyond the limits of the rational, linear thinking upon which we tend to rely.

In the expressive arts our focus is always on process over product. The purpose of the creative exploration is not to create something beautiful but to engage in the experience as a prayer and an opportunity to witness the unfolding of the creative act.

The arts are especially powerful in this work with archetypes because it helps us access symbolic language and image to more fully understand the invitations of each archetype to us.

WORKING WITH MANDALAS

For your visual exploration, you will be working with mandala-making in a variety of forms. The word *mandala* is Sanskrit for circle, and mandalas appear across cultures. We find them in rose windows, labyrinths, the Celtic cross, ancient stone circles, rosaries, spirals, and those beautiful sand mandalas created by Buddhist monks only to later be destroyed, symbolizing the transitory nature of life. Hildegard of Bingen had many visions in the shape of a mandala.

Carl Jung, in his work with his patients, began to notice that when they had dreams with circles in them, the circles were always symbols of wholeness. He began his own practice of daily mandala drawing as a way to give space for his experience on the page before him. He saw them as representations of the unconscious and therefore a field of inner exploration. He wrote:

> When I began drawing the mandalas, however, I saw that everything, all the paths I had been following, all the steps I had taken were leading back to a single point—

> namely, to the mid-point. It became increasingly plain to
> me that the mandala is the center. It is the exponent of
> all paths. It is the path to the center, to individuation. . .
> . I began to understand that the goal of psychic develop-
> ment is the self. There is no linear evolution, only a cir-
> cumambulation of the self. Uniform development exists,
> at most, only at the beginning; later, everything points
> toward the center. . . . I knew that in finding the mandala
> as an expression of the self I had attained what was for
> me the ultimate.[3]

Mandalas also act as sacred containers for our process. Having boundaries for our inner work is essential to being able to
dive deeply into previously unexplored territory. The container
is created in many ways—by the form of art itself, by our own
preparation for the time of creating and making sure there are no
disruptions, and by having someone else witness what we have
created in a loving and compassionate way.

You will need some supplies for the mandala explorations. For
coloring in the mandala forms, you will want to make a copy
of the mandala template in the book (or download it from
AbbeyoftheArts.com) and a set of colored pencils, crayons, or
markers. For drawing the mandalas in the gush art form, you will
also use these colored drawing materials and some plain paper.
Collage requires a source of images, which can be old magazines,
catalogs, or even used art books, plus a glue stick, a pair of scissors,
and a round piece of paper to which you will adhere the images.
For the photography explorations, any camera will do, even the
one on your phone. We will also explore working with sand, once
at a sandy place like the beach and once with colored sand to create a mandala. You can purchase multi-packs of different colored
sand in art and craft supply stores. And for our final exploration,
we will work with natural materials found outdoors in a park, seashore, or other hiking path.

HOW TO WORK WITH THIS BOOK

This book is a journey through your inner life. I recommended you move through it slowly. You don't have to go in order of the chapters. Feel free to read over the table of contents and see if one calls to you especially and begin there.

Consider allowing a week per chapter or even a month so there is time to reflect and integrate the materials. Gather with a group and go through a season together or a whole year. The reflections and meditations are meant to be engaged and integrated into your own life experience, not just read. The transformation and insight comes through immersing yourself in the process suggested.

You can also choose which of the ways of engaging the material call most to you at this time. While it is wonderful to offer yourself the multi-sensory experience of reading, reflecting, meditating, creating visual art, moving, writing, and poetry, perhaps there is one of these that most supports your journey right now. Tune into what you most need for your own support.

Francis of Assisi: The Fool

INTRODUCTION TO FRANCIS OF ASSISI

St. Francis (1181/1182–1226) is perhaps one of the most well-loved saints in the Christian tradition. Although we may have more of a Hallmark-card image of him as the birdbath Francis, always surrounded by animals with a look of peaceful bliss, he was also a saint who challenged the status quo.

Francis was one of those rowdy young men, much like St. Ignatius of Loyola, who was brought up in a very wealthy Italian family, had a life of parties, spent time daydreaming of becoming a knight, and then was sent off to fight in battle as a soldier. Captured, he began having visions while held in prison and returned home a different man.

Soon after his return Francis passed a leper, who previously would have caused him to turn away, but instead, he saw Jesus in this encounter and embraced and kissed the man. This encounter had a powerful effect on him and led him to renounce his great wealth and turn to a life of service. One day in the church of San Damiano, right outside of Assisi, he heard this invitation from Jesus: "Francis, rebuild my church which you see is falling into ruins." Francis's spontaneous response was a hearty yes, and he gathered a group of brothers together to achieve this.

In order to raise money to rebuild the church, he stole cloth and a horse from his father. His father was furious at this betrayal and dragged Francis in front of the bishop, who demanded that Francis repay his father. At this, Francis stripped himself naked and handed his clothes and the money over to his father, declaring that God was now the only father he recognized. He was given a rough tunic to wear. This Christ-like poverty was a radical notion at the time as the church reveled in riches and wealth.

Soon Francis gathered followers around him. He went from village to village preaching a new way of following the Gospel and even was found preaching to the animals. This earned him the nickname "God's fool." Francis once said to a cardinal who was overseeing a gathering of the friars: "I do not want to hear any mention of the rule of St. Augustine, of St. Bernard, or of St. Benedict. The Lord has told me that he wanted to make a new fool of me." He was not so much rejecting these earlier rules as claiming his authority to make something new, something that may seem foolish to the ways of the world.

In chapter 9 of his First Rule, Francis wrote of his monks, "They should be glad to live among social outcasts." This reminds me of a saying by the desert father Abba Nilus: "Happy is the monk who thinks he is the outcast of all." The outcast is the one who doesn't fit neatly into mainstream society. When we commit to the contemplative path, we are called to spaciousness and presence rather than rushing and productivity, choosing a simple life in the midst of an abundance of riches, and rejecting the pervasive consumer message. To be an outcast means that we don't align ourselves with the dominant way of thinking.

Francis was a man who loved living life on the "edges" of things. Rejecting power, prestige, and wealth, he found freedom and joy in the simplicity of his path. Walking away from security he found new purpose. He lived out the gospel "preferential option for the poor" and was drawn to those who lived on the margins, the poor and sick, just as Jesus did. He washed the bodies of lepers who were literally outcasts—people were forbidden to touch them.

Ultimately, what he was living out was a profoundly incarnational spirituality, which demands that we look at the world differently. It means that everything in our lives is alive with the sacred presence if only we commit ourselves to seeing anew. As we strive on the spiritual path for greater and greater heights, this may at first seem like a disappointment. Even after months of contemplative practice, we are called to encounter the divine in diapers and disappointments, preparing breakfast and commuting to work, in times of illness and grief, in the person who annoys us, and in the person we don't even notice because we have turned away so many times.

In his famous poem "Canticle of the Creatures" where he praises the creatures and the constellations, the four elements of earth, water, wind, and fire, he even calls bodily death "Sister" because he recognizes her as friend in this life, as a reminder of what is essential. He composed this work a year before he died when he was nearly blind and growing more blind each day. Although no longer able to see, he described nature as a theophany, a place of divine encounter and intimate relationship. The canticle is a celebration of the incarnation through all of creation.

Francis calls us to an alternative way of being, to consider what responsibilities weigh us down and how we might discover more freedom. He invites us to dance on the edges of the world and find there the beauty of what is most central.

ICON SYMBOLISM: FRANCIS OF ASSISI

The quote "the world is my monastery" (sometimes translated as "the world is my cloister") is attributed to St. Francis. He is pictured in his traditional brown robe and with the tonsure, a sign of his commitment to poverty. Francis is dancing out in the fields with some of his animal companions, including the salmon, the fox, and the birds. The church behind him is in the process of being built because he was given the call to "rebuild." I invite you to look with "soft eyes" upon the icon, eyes ready to receive rather than take, and open your heart up to whatever gifts may come from this time of prayer.

THE ARCHETYPE OF THE FOOL

"We are fools for the sake of Christ" (1 Cor 4:10). We have explored many aspects of Francis's foolishness: stripping his clothing publicly, appearing naked in the church, renouncing his wealth, befriending all creatures, and calling his community of brothers "fools for Christ," reflecting the words of St. Paul above. He tames a wolf, and during the Crusades, he walks unarmed across the Egyptian desert into the sultan's camp where he had every reason to expect his own death, a foolish act indeed.

We are always being called to new revelation and to see the world from another perspective. The inner Fool is the one who helps us to see things anew and to dismantle the accepted wisdom of our times. Paul also writes, "Has not God made foolish the wisdom of the world?" (1 Cor 1:20). Productivity, striving, consumption, and speed are some of the false gods of our Western culture. A life committed to following the divine path is one that makes the world's wisdom seem foolish, but conversely, the world often looks upon those with spiritual commitment as the ones who are "fools."

This can be a challenging archetype for some of us as we often try to do everything possible so as not to look foolish. However, this archetype is the one that helps to subvert the dominant paradigm of acceptable ways of thinking and living. The author G. K. Chesterton, in his book about Francis of Assisi, explores the idea of Francis seeing the world upside down, which is really seeing it right side up, because we get a totally new perspective. There is a subversive act of truth-telling through the Fool's humor and playfulness.

The Fool risks mockery by stepping out of socially acceptable roles and asks, where are we willing to look foolish? Through the Fool we find vicarious release for much we have repressed in ourselves. If we have always lived according to the "rules" or been overly concerned with how things look, the Fool invites us to break loose and play. The Fool encourages us to laugh at ourselves, reminding us that humor and humility have the same root, the Latin word *humus*, which means earth or ground.

By ignoring predictable or conventional behavior we encounter a fresh perspective. The Fool also helps to reveal the hypocrisies of life. For example, a king often had a court jester to help him see things differently and bring his ego in check. In modern times, founder of the Christian social justice magazine *Sojourners*, Jim Wallis, called Jon Stewart, when he was host of *The Daily Show*, the modern equivalent of the court jester, a companion to the Fool.

The Concise Oxford Dictionary of World Religions says that "holy fools subvert prevailing orthodoxy and orthopraxis in order to point to the truth which lies beyond immediate conformity." The sacred function of the Fool is to tear down the illusions we hold so dear and illuminate what is new through playfulness and humor, using shocking or unconventional behavior to challenge the status quo or social norms. The Fool helps us to see beyond the dualities we live by.

We activate the Fool when we do something that others have a hard time understanding or accepting. I remember when John and I first began our move to Europe, and we sold off or gave away our possessions. Various family members and friends couldn't

understand different things we had let go of—how could we release our library of treasured books? How could I burn years of
journals? How could John quit his secure job? To some, our choices appeared "foolish" because they didn't fit their way of thinking
about how you move through life. To others, they seemed liberat-
ing precisely because it was a different path chosen.

The Russian Church has a special word for saints who are
regarded as holy fools: *yurodivi*. These are the wild souls who witness to other possibilities.

The Fool raises our insecurities. Can we risk showing up wearing the "wrong clothes" or nothing at all? There is an absolute
vulnerability when we do something we know won't be accepted
by others. As we lock out the world with our keys and our plans,
the Fool challenges us to see life differently.

The Fool has nothing to lose, does not cling to anything, has
nothing for someone to steal. The Fool for Christ, says Eastern
Orthodox Metropolitan Kallistos Ware, "has no possessions, no
family, no position, and so can speak with a prophetic boldness."

THE SHADOW SIDE OF THE FOOL

As with all the archetypes, when the Fool's energy is not allowed,
it is suppressed in the unconscious and comes out in other, often
destructive ways. We find the shadow Fool when we use humor
to tear people down or when we find ourselves moving toward
cynicism rather than a constructive criticism of world problems.

The shadow Fool delights in breaking rules, regardless of the
consequences, just for the sake of it, rather than to reveal a truth.
The Fool in shadow form can also reject all the conventional
norms of society without finding a balance of challenge and what
needs to be done for self-preservation.

JESUS AND THE FOOL ARCHETYPE: THE PARABLE OF THE WORKERS IN THE VINEYARD
REFLECTION BY JOHN VALTERS PAINTNER

"Take what belongs to you and go; I choose to give to this last the same as I give to you. Am I not allowed to do what I choose with what belongs to me? Or are you envious because I am generous?" So the last will be first, and the first will be last.

—Matthew 20:14–16

Begin by reading the whole scripture passage and then pray with the excerpt in a contemplative way such as lectio divina (see guidelines in the appendix).

Jesus offers us this parable of the Holy Fool, the one who subverts the way things are done and confounds our expectations. Jesus sat at table with tax collectors and prostitutes. He healed on the Sabbath. He broke boundaries, turned things upside down, and invites us to do the same.

Conventional wisdom would say that the landowner of the vineyard is a foolish one. He was foolish not to hire enough workers, more than once. The landowner hires laborers at five different times throughout the day. That certainly seems a foolish waste of his valuable time.

Then the landowner is also foolish to pay those laborers who only worked part of the day the same standard wage as those who worked the entire day. Surely those hired last would not have expected a standard, full-day's pay. The landowner is throwing money away when he doesn't need to. He even foolishly jeopardizes his relationship with the labor force by paying equal wages for unequal work.

Conventional wisdom would also go on to answer that the laborers who are hired first have just cause to feel as if they've been made fools of by the landowner. If he has the resources to pay a full day's wage to laborers who only put in a few hours of work, surely he could pay those laborers who put in more work a higher wage.

But when the landowner is confronted by the laborers who were hired earlier in the day, he adds insult to injury when he turns the tables on them. He contends that he did these laborers no wrong. He paid them what they agreed to be paid for the work they agreed to do. What is it to them if he pays others the same wage for less work? What right do they have to tell him what to do with his money?

The underlying question that Jesus is asking in this parable is, why be jealous or upset about the success of someone else, particularly when you have enough? Everyone is paid because everyone was given work.

And isn't that the real motivation of the landowner? The parable states he goes out and sees others standing idle. The landowner doesn't hire them because he needs more laborers; he hires them because they need work and the wage it brings.

It is a foolish business model, as viewed from today's standards. But the landowner is not thinking in terms of the laws of economics. He is thinking in terms of the Laws of the Covenant, one of which is to share one's wealth with those in need (see Leviticus 19:9 and 23:22 and Deuteronomy 24:19).

Ultimately God's ways are not our own. Our expectations will be disappointed again and again if we go by conventional terms. The Fool invites us to embrace the One whose logic goes against our preconceived ideas, inviting us into an upside-down world governed by love.

THE PRACTICE OF HUMILITY

The Fool calls us to remember our own earthiness, to know that one day Sister Death will visit us as well. The desert monks and St. Benedict also counseled "remember daily that one day you will die." In embracing this truth we can find freedom. We begin to take ourselves and the weight of our concerns less seriously.

"Be humble" is a call that might raise your hackles a bit. I know it does for me. Humility can be used to subjugate those whose voices we do not want to hear. Or we can take on false humility and act as though we are not full of pride as a way to increase our standing.

Esther de Waal describes the practice of humility as recognizing that I am "profoundly earthed." To do this I only need ponder all the ways I am reliant on the earth for provision of food and air and sunlight. Humility reminds us that we have limitations and we can't take on everything, which also enables us to commit to something and do it very well.

Humility is really a dance between embracing our limits and our giftedness. It means finding humor in our shortcomings and foibles and learning to take ourselves less seriously. But it also means seeing the world through this lens and learning to see things from another perspective.

The Fool finds liberation in humility because concerns over how we will appear are set aside for an expression of the deep truths of our soul. In connecting with our inner Fools we are able to risk seeming foolish in service of freeing ourselves to follow what is most essential. Humility can help illuminate the way ahead.

MEDITATION: INVITING YOUR INNER FOOL

Find a comfortable seat, and take a few moments to settle into your body. Become aware of places of tightness and holding, and breathe into those places, shifting in any way needed to bring ease.

Allow your breath to deepen and bring you to a still point within. Imagine drawing your awareness down to your heart center and resting there for a few moments as you connect to what your experience is in this moment. Just let yourself have whatever feelings are rising up, without trying to change them.

From this heart-centered place invite Francis to be present with you in this time of prayer. Welcome him in and notice how he is dressed. See his mannerisms and expressions. Spend a few moments connecting with his presence and then welcoming in the Spirit to be present as well with you both.

Ask Francis and the Spirit to help show you your own inner Fool. As you drop inward, see if you might release to a playful open-hearted quality. Breathe in the gift of humility and feel the tender weight of your own earthiness.

Ask to be shown the places of life that you perhaps take too seriously. What creates tension for you? Where do you feel constricted?

Open yourself to seeing what conventions of your life need some challenge. Where are the places you are most afraid of looking foolish? Can you invite Francis, the Spirit, and the archetypal energy of the inner Fool to be with you gently here?

Then let the places of embarrassment shimmer forth. What in your life makes you blush at the thought? When have been the moments when you have felt most embarrassed? Allow these to be shown to you and notice if there are any patterns.

Sit for a while with these images and then ask what most hinders you from taking seriously your inner gifts and dreams. What are the obstacles that feel too difficult? The people's opinions you take most seriously or whom you don't want to disappoint? Just allow this to unfold as well.

When you feel ready to close this time of prayer, ask for a gift, a symbol of some kind to carry with you back to the outer world. Once this becomes clear, let it move into a gesture in your body. Then let your breath carry you back to the room and spend some time writing any insights or experiences you want to remember.

MANDALA EXPLORATION: COLORING MANDALAS

For your first exploration in working with mandalas I invite you to gather some colored pens, pencils, crayons, or markers. Whatever coloring materials you might have are just fine. You can download a full-page version of the mandala from AbbeyoftheArts.com or make a copy of the one here. These mandalas come from artist Stacy Wills.

There is something about allowing ourselves the gift of coloring, like we did when we were children, that can tap into a place of carefree innocence, much like what the Fool offers to the world.

When beginning any creative exploration, it is important to create a sacred space within which to work. Turn off the phone and e-mail notifications, light a candle, find some time when you will not be disturbed by others, and put a sign on your door if necessary. Decide if you want to play quiet music or just lean into the silence.

Awakening your energy through gentle movement can be help-ful. Consider putting on a song, perhaps one that feels playful to you or resonant with the Fool's energy, and just let yourself move in response to the music. This can be very helpful in moving out of your head and down into your body and heart space.

Allow a few moments to pause first and connect to your breath by allowing a few deep inhales and exhales. Then just become aware of the grace you seek in this time. It may be as simple as "I seek the grace of freedom to enter in without inner judgment or criticism" or something like "I seek the grace of allowing my inner Fool to speak to me in new ways, to listen for the invitations." Just tune into what you need for yourself.

As you move through the time of creating, become aware of any voices that arise that might interfere with or undermine your process. Honor their presence and then gently let them go, re-turning to your breath as an anchor and way of staying focused on the process of creation.

Let this time of creating be a prayer, a communication with God who is always infusing whatever we do. Invite the Spirit into this time of coloring as a way of opening yourself to whatever wisdom wants to emerge. After centering yourself through breath and prayer, notice if there is a color that chooses you from the variety of possibilities. As you tap into your inner Fool, notice which color sparks your heart and begin there.

When you have completed the coloring, rest for a few minutes with the mandala in front of you. Gently return to your breath, and simply behold the image, which means to look with a receptive gaze. You aren't trying to figure anything out here; just be with what has come forth in this time.

At the end of each creative exploration, I highly recommend allowing some time to journal. Notice the process—what happened while you were creating, what feelings and judgments rose up—and dialogue with the colors and images that emerged.

FOR REFLECTION

- What about Francis's story most inspires or energizes you? Where do you feel the strongest connection or disconnection?
- What concrete steps toward holy foolishness can you make in your life?
- Where in your life do you feel called to something but are afraid of the risk of looking like a fool?
- How might you practice humility and this sense of being profoundly earthed in your life?
- What did the visual art exploration experience reveal to you?

CLOSING BLESSING

The poem below was inspired by my own imagining what it would be like to hang out with Francis in an Irish pub, which is a place of connection and merriment. I can see him completely at home and making everyone else feel at ease by the sheer joy, openness, and utter foolishness of his presence.

St. Francis at the Corner Pub

Approaching the door, you can already
hear his generous laughter.

He stands on the bar upside down for a moment
to get a new perspective on things,

a flash of polka-dotted boxers
as his brown robe cascades over his head,

sandaled toes wiggling in the air in time with
a fiddle playing in the corner.

Rain falls heavily in the deepening darkness
and he orders a round of drinks

despite his vow of poverty and the single silver coin
in his pocket, multiplied by the last Guinness poured.

Nothing like a good glass of wine, he gleefully says,
heavy Italian accent echoing through the room,

he holds it up to the overhead light, pausing for a moment
lost in its crimson splendor, breathes deeply.

At ease among fishmongers and plumbers,
widows and college students, and the

single mother sneaking out for a moment
of freedom from colic, cries, and diapers.

As the wind blows rain sideways, in come the
animals, *benvenuti* to pigeons, squirrels, seagulls, crows,

and the neighborhood cat balding from mange,
a chorus of yowls, coos, caws, and meows arising,

all huddle around him. No one objects to the growing
menagerie, just glad to be dry and warm.

He clinks glasses all around, no one left out.

May you continue to discover the delight of holy foolishness, and may Francis and the Fool guide you to new perspectives and possibilities. May joy and laughter illuminate the way ahead.

King David: The Sovereign

INTRODUCTION TO KING DAVID

What first draws me to David is the story of him dancing through the streets. The scriptures tell us that "David danced before the LORD with all his might" (2 Sm 6:14). The occasion was the Ark of the Covenant being brought into Jerusalem. I love this image of the kingly figure abandoning himself to joy. Even his wife Michal looks on him with scorn for behaving in such an "un-kingly" way. And yet, here is perhaps where we see a bit of the Fool in David and his willingness to appear foolish for God in celebration.

David was born the youngest of eight sons to the shepherd Jesse of Bethlehem and was anointed king of the yet to be established Kingdom of Israel by the Prophet Samuel who was sent in secret. At the time, Saul was still technically king, but he had lost favor with God due to his many sins and willfulness. David was told to keep quiet until the time was right.

Young David became a servant of Saul's. He played his harp and sang to soothe the troubled soul of Saul, who had frequent emotional bouts of rage. The texts tell us, "And whenever the evil spirit from God came upon Saul, David took the lyre and played it with his hand, and Saul would be relieved and feel better, and the evil spirit would depart from him" (1 Sm 16:23).

The young David famously slayed the Philistine giant, Goliath, with a single stone from his slingshot. Thus David became a champion in Saul's army, leading many successful campaigns against the Israelite's enemies. Saul tried to have David killed by sending him on dangerous missions with the promise of his daughter Michal's hand in marriage. Saul's plan backfired: David was victorious and became the king's son-in-law. But still jealous of David's growing fame, Saul sought to persecute David. David became a fugitive but continued to fight on behalf of his people.

Saul's son, Jonathan, and David became the best of friends. Jonathan tried to balance loyalty to his friend while honoring his father. Nevertheless, Jonathan helped David escape Saul's persecution.

When Saul and Jonathan died in battle, David took the throne. He was eventually able to defeat the Philistines and establish the Kingdom of Israel. David captured the walled city of Jerusalem and made it his capital. David danced before the Ark of the Covenant when he brought it to Jerusalem, its new home on what would become the Temple Mount, in a triumphal procession. David's son Solomon succeeded him and built the Temple to permanently house the Ark.

David was a multi-faceted character. Unlike the hagiographies of saints that tend to leave out the darker aspects of their personalities, the Hebrew scriptures offer us a wide array of figures with their shadows and struggles, as well as triumphs and victories. I appreciate reading about the full spectrum of human experience in these scripture stories.

We see some of this shadow at work when David had an affair with Bathsheba and she became pregnant. David arranged to have Bathsheba's husband, Uriah, killed in battle to cover up the affair. But the prophet Nathan confronted David about his sins, and David expresses his repentance by writing what we know today as Psalm 51.

In it David prays, "Create a clean heart in me, O God." It is a beautiful expression of regret and taking responsibility for his actions. As Sovereign, he sought forgiveness to restore things to their rightful order through prayer. This is a sign of a good king (or queen), not that mistakes won't happen but to seek restitution when the truth is revealed and to take responsibility for choices made.

Then there was the family drama when David's eldest son, Amnon, raped his half-sister, Tamar. David did not punish Amnon harshly enough for Tamar's full-brother, Absalom, so Absalom murdered Amnon. David again did not harshly punish his offspring, so Absalom, having lost all faith in his father, attempted a coup to depose him. Despite King David's orders, his son Absalom was killed in the ensuing rebellion.

David had several sons by his many wives, but Bathsheba was his favorite wife. Even though her son Solomon was not the oldest or next in line, Queen Bathsheba schemed to have her son Solomon named as David's heir upon the king's death.

The mighty warrior and poet King David lived long enough to become a feeble old man. Solomon succeeded him as king, but it was not a completely smooth or bloodless transition.

As king, David had many triumphs. He united the Kingdom of Israel and restored the Ark of the Covenant to Jerusalem. He was a complicated character, just as we all are. His motivations were often mixed.

ICON SYMBOLISM: KING DAVID

The quote on the icon comes from 2 Samuel in the Hebrew scriptures, where it says that "David danced before the LORD with all his might" in front of the Ark of the Covenant. The Ark is seen behind him being carried through the streets.

King David is depicted wearing a simple garment and playing a harp. The psalms are attributed to him as poet and musician.

I invite you to allow a few moments to gaze upon this icon and see what David reveals to you in this image.

THE ARCHETYPE OF THE SOVEREIGN

There is a story about Sir Gawain and Lady Ragnell that expresses the heart of sovereignty well. Sir Gawain must decide whether he wants Lady Ragnell to remain beautiful by day and ugly by night, or the other way around. He finally decides to leave the choice up to her and thereby grants her sovereignty over herself. She remains beautiful all the time.

Sovereignty is about being centered in your own power and taking full responsibility for meeting your needs. Sovereignty sounds archaic in some ways, and yet it is one of the archetypal energies we find within us. The reason so many myths and fairy tales speak of kings and queens is that these figures reflect back something of ourselves.

Sovereignty is in many ways a midlife word. We don't really begin to live into our own power until we have grown wise enough to recognize our limitations as well. In her book *Queen of Myself: Stepping Into Sovereignty at Midlife*, Donna Henes suggests that the traditional stages of maiden, mother, and crone for women are incomplete as women's lifespans get longer. She suggests the addition of the queen or sovereign archetype between mother and crone as a time to really live into a sense of your own power. In the book *King, Warrior, Magician, and Lover*, Robert Moore describes the king as a primal energy in men's spirituality as well.

The Sovereign is not a victim of life. Another favorite story is that of Persephone who was abducted into the Underworld by

Hades. She ate the pomegranate seeds that end up requiring her to stay there for part of the year. She became queen, a movement from her victim role to stepping into her own power and fullness.

The Sovereign accepts full responsibility for his or her choices. One of our central questions in life is, what is my task in this world? Living into what that is may take a lifetime, but the Sovereign helps us to claim the call that is our birthright and step into life with confidence. That gift is then offered with joy as a blessing to the world. No apologies need to be made for offering this essential contribution. Our inner Sovereign knows that the world will not be complete without our part of the greater vision. We participate in the co-creation of a more just and beautiful future each in our own unique way. We manifest the Sovereign's energy through centeredness, confidence, and calmness.

When I live from my inner Sovereign, I act out of a sense of agency that is a willingness to take action on my own behalf for the benefit of others, to exert my power or influence. This is not what we think we should be doing for others, but it emerges from the very deep and wise place within us. My task is never determined by "shoulds" or shame. I take full responsibility for choosing this path, and there is a sacramental quality to it as a response to a holy calling.

When we are living fully from our inner Sovereign, we embody a calm and assertive energy. The archetype of the Sovereign manifests strength, centeredness, security, stability, vitality, and joy. It is the part of us that overcomes the disorder and chaos of life, allowing creativity to arise from places that feel difficult or challenging. Sovereigns rule from their true Self, the deepest and wisest parts of their being. There they listen to the holy stirrings within already. The Sovereign calls us to fully claim our path in ways that are not anxious but steady and sure.

A true Sovereign blesses others by his or her presence. When we live into our own power in healthy and life-giving ways, we witness to a different way of being that empowers those around us. When we encounter someone who is deeply in touch with their Sovereign, regardless of their wealth or status in the world, we listen because they are in touch with their own wisdom and are not afraid to speak it aloud. Sovereigns create safe and healthy spaces for others to grow and develop their gifts and are never threatened by others living into their own power as well. Our world needs people of maturity, centeredness, wisdom, and peace to help us move into the next phase of our evolution together.

THE SHADOW SIDE OF THE SOVEREIGN

The shadow side of the Sovereign is revealed in the Tyrant wielding power over others. Healthy humility is an essential aspect of the Sovereign, so when that is absent we see the shadow emerge and over-identification with power for its own sake. Is there a tyrannical aspect to one of your inner selves? A voice that shuts out all others? The Sovereign is the source of our desire and movement toward greatness, but the shadow side can come through inflation and grandiosity. We have to recognize our proper relationship to this power.

Another shadow side is the Martyr who often lives out of a false humility. When we don't take responsibility for meeting our own needs and living fully in the world, we may start to feel resentful of others as we rely on them to meet our needs. We may resent someone who is living a full, glorious, and powerful life because it is what we so desperately long for. Are there times when you criticize someone else's gifts because of your own misplaced sense of responsibility? How do you seek approval from other people before taking care of yourself? Do you deny yourself pleasures of life out of a misguided sense of sacrifice or unworthiness? Do you hold back on your enjoyment of life?

●●

JESUS AND THE SOVEREIGN ARCHETYPE: ENTERING JERUSALEM
REFLECTION BY JOHN VALTERS PAINTNER

Then they brought it to Jesus, and after throwing their cloaks on the colt, they set Jesus on it. As he rode along, people kept spreading their cloaks on the road. As he was now approaching the path down from the Mount of Olives, the whole multitude of the disciples began to praise God joyfully with a loud voice for all the deeds of power that they had seen, saying, "Blessed is the king who comes in the name of the Lord!"

—Luke 19:29–40

Begin by reading the whole scripture passage as indicated and then pray with the excerpt in a contemplative way such as lectio divina (see guidelines in the appendix).

Jesus is on his way to Jerusalem. His disciples are worried. They know that Jesus has had enough run-ins with the Jerusalem religious authorities to be justifiably concerned about their safety. Jesus decides to go anyway. Jesus knows that going to Jerusalem will likely mean his death. He makes the sacrifice all the same.

Just before reaching the Holy City of David, Jesus sends two disciples ahead to procure an animal for him to ride on into the city. On the surface, it's an unusual request for one who has walked all over Judea. There is no other reference to Jesus and animals in the gospels. (Even the image of the pregnant Mary riding a donkey to Bethlehem for the census isn't actually in the Bible.) But here, Jesus makes an exception to fulfill an ancient prophesy about the Messiah. He's using the common knowledge of scrip-

ture to make a statement. Jesus doesn't need to come out and say
he is the Messiah when he can show everyone.

Jesus is called (among other names and titles) Lord Jesus Christ,
Son of God, and Prince of Peace. And yet, I don't often associate
the humble Messiah, Jesus of Nazareth, with being royalty. His
father, Joseph, was of the House of King David. But so were so
many others at that time (the Tree of Jesse had branched much
in the centuries following David's reign), and Joseph was but one
branch, a simple carpenter from a small, back-water village. The
Magi, following a star and the ancient prophecies of a new king,
prostrated themselves before the infant Jesus and offered gifts fit
for a king. Did it ever occur to the Magi that they might find the
infant they sought in a manger?

Jesus certainly did not have a royal upbringing. The scriptures
state that Jesus grew up like any other child, after a brief period as
a refugee. As much as Joseph and Mary must have loved their son,
did they think of Jesus as an heir to a throne?

Even once Jesus begins his public ministry and proclaims the
Kingdom of God, he walked among the common people. Jesus'
circle of influence and audience was not the rich and powerful;
they were often the targets of his preaching. And so I find it difficult, despite the titles, to think of Jesus as royalty. His disciples
call Jesus "teacher" and eventually "Messiah," but did any of them
think of their friend as their king?

Toward the end of his ministry, Jesus knew that the authorities
wanted to silence him. The disciples warned Jesus that going to
Jerusalem was dangerous. Yet Jesus also knew the ancient prophecies about the Messiah. And so in what I consider a move to be
a bit uncharacteristic, Jesus sends two disciples to fetch for him
a donkey on which to ride triumphantly into the royal city of
Jerusalem. No exchange of money is mentioned, and the only ex-

planation is simply that "the Lord needs it." How did the animal's owner react to the taking of the animal?

The pretense for Jesus' arrest is that Jesus was claiming to be a king and plotting to challenge Caesar. Jesus is questioned about it at his trial. The soldiers who torture Jesus dress him up in a "royal" cape and a crown of thorns. They laugh at him. The Jewish high priests complain about the inscription over Jesus' crucifix, wanting it to say that Jesus "claimed" to be the King of the Jews. Certainly, none of these people believed that Jesus was a sovereign of any kind. In his lifetime, did anyone think of Jesus as royalty?

In this passage, Jesus owns his sovereignty. He gives orders and claims what he needs. It is an image of Jesus that goes against my standard humble Messiah. I rarely think of Jesus as the Prince of Peace, not because I don't think of him as peaceful but because I don't often think of him as royal. It is my own baggage that keeps me from embracing this archetype. For even Christ, when the time is right, takes command and issues orders. He knows when to take charge and how to proceed decisively. It is what needs to be done because the time is at hand.

THE PRACTICE OF BLESSING EACH MOMENT

One of the beautiful practices of both the Celtic and Jewish imagination is blessing the world, blessing each and every encounter, experience, every ordinary moment. In the Jewish worldview, each act becomes worthy of blessing. Gratitude is offered for all gifts: upon awakening, when crossing a threshold, when eating a meal, and when lighting candles. The Talmud calls for one hundred blessings each day.

The kitchen is a holy place, the office is a sanctuary, the bedroom is a place of divine revelation, and the world at our feet shimmers brightly each moment if we only have eyes to see. God is with us moment by moment and blessings remind us of this truth.

This act of blessing is really a special way of paying attention. It is a moment of remembering wonder as our primary response to the world. It is an act of consecrating the day.

It is also a way of honoring our own gifts in the world as blessing. When we claim our inner Sovereign, we make no apologies for sharing our unique treasures. We do so freely, knowing others will be blessed by this, just as we are blessed by their sharing.

Photography is an especially accessible art medium in our modern world, where almost everyone carries a camera built into their phone or small, portable cameras with good picture quality are widely available. In my book *Eyes of the Heart: Photography as a Christian Contemplative Practice*, I suggest ways to engage your camera as a tool for prayer and to cultivate a different way of seeing the world. "Eyes of the heart" refers to a kind of graced vision that is focused more on receiving gifts than on "taking" photos. Seeing in this way is different from our ordinary way of scanning our field of vision for the information we want to find. Instead, it is a spacious gaze that savors each moment.

In the Benedictine monastic tradition, everything is considered sacred. The stranger at the door is to be welcomed in as Christ. The kitchen utensils are to be treated just like the altar vessels. The hinges of the day call us to remember the presence of God again and again so that time becomes a cascade of prayers.

So what if I imagine my eyes as a vessel of blessing? What if I moved through the day, and each time I felt drawn to take out my camera, I paused before pushing the button and consecrated what I was gazing upon?

Perhaps I might even say a short prayer: "Bless this shimmering moment, may my eyes receive its gifts, may my heart open ever wider in response." You might craft your own holy words.

In this way, our photography can become an act of deepened awareness and love. We can begin to see all the everyday things of our lives as openings into the depth dimension of the world: the steam rising from my coffee, the bird singing from a tree branch outside my window, the doorbell announcing a friend's arrival, and the meal that nourishes my body for service. Each of these moments invites us to pause and to see it through a different kind of vision. And my practice of photography is a way to reinforce this kind of vision in all aspects of my life.

Consecrate the day with your camera. Even without a camera, bless the world with your eyes. Offer gratitude for every ordinary gift. Embracing the Sovereign is to know the goodness of the entire kingdom and affirming that in every way possible.

MEDITATION: INVITING YOUR INNER SOVEREIGN

Begin by allowing some time to center yourself through attention to your breath. Let your breath draw your awareness inward, growing increasingly still. As you slowly drop down to your heart space, invite King David to be with you in this meditation experience. Welcome in his presence and notice how he appears to you in dress and personality. Allow some time to be with him in this way, simply growing familiar with his presence. Then welcome in the Spirit to be present with you as well.

Ask David to show you your inner Sovereign. Let your breath continue to draw you more deeply inward, and open yourself to the king or queen within you. Welcome in the sense of confidence and assuredness in yourself that the Sovereign brings. Imagine your Sovereign blessing the world around you.

Ask to be shown the places of your life where you are being asked to claim greater responsibility for your actions. Where have you abdicated your own power in the world to others and failed to share your gifts freely because of shame or laziness? Allow these moments to be shown to you and receive them as gifts and insights for your journey.

Sit with whatever images unfold and stay present. Then ask for a gift of some kind, something to symbolize your inner Sovereign and the power and grace you have to offer the world. Allow time for this to be revealed as well. Once you see it, let it move into your body and express it through a gesture. Then let your breath carry you gently back to the room and write down anything you want to make note of.

MANDALA EXPLORATION: COLORING MANDALAS

The Sovereign archetype is associated especially with the symbol of the mandala, the sacred circle that holds the center and is a symbol of wholeness. The Sovereign dwells in our own center and is our source of power for action in the world. You are invited to once again pray with mandalas through coloring as a way to meditate on the ways you feel centered and powerful in the world.

As you did in your work with coloring mandalas and the Fool, begin by gathering your supplies: a copy of the mandala pattern and some colored drawing implements. You can download a full-page version of the mandala from AbbeyoftheArts.com or make a copy of the one on page 28. The Sovereign makes no apologies for taking time to nourish him- or herself through creative activities.

Create the sacred space needed by turning off distractions and lighting a candle to symbolize your desire to invite in the Spirit to be present with you in this time. You can play music or rest into the silence.

You might awaken your energy again through gentle movement, playing a song resonant with the king or queen, and just allowing a few minutes to let your body explore and stretch.

When you are ready to move into the coloring, connect to your breath, draw your awareness to your center, and then name the grace you seek in this experience. Perhaps your desire is to let this time be a prayer or to be mindful of each moment as it unfolds. As critical voices arise during the process, simply let them go.

Invite the Spirit into this time of coloring as a way of opening yourself to whatever wisdom wants to emerge. As you begin exploring the energy of the Sovereign through color, notice which shade or hue calls to you first and follow that impulse.

When you are finished with your coloring, simply gaze with love on the image for a few moments, just being with what has emerged. When you feel ready, journal about the process and what you experienced.

FOR REFLECTION

- What about King David's story most inspires or energizes you? Where do you feel the strongest connection or disconnection?

- What concrete steps toward sovereignty can you make in your life?
- How are you being called to take responsibility for your fulfillment in life and your choices? Consider also the un-conscious choices you make that keep you from spending as much time on your passion as you'd love.
- What is the deepest thing you feel called toward—the one you feel passionate about and you know is profoundly true? How can you live this out in the world without apology or pretense?
- What is the crown you are being called to wear?
- How might you practice blessing the world?
- What did the visual art exploration experience reveal to you about your inner Sovereign?

CLOSING BLESSING

King David is known as one of the writers of the great book of Hebrew poetry, the Psalms, which has been used in prayer for thousands of years by both Jews and Christians. In writing this poem I imagined writing it as a "lost psalm" by David, a prayer exploring the vagaries of the human heart. David is such a real and interesting character in the scriptures. He is the proud leader and unifier of the people and a murderous warrior. He is one who danced and wrote poetry and also is known for his many acts of adultery. I wanted the poem to identify with this inner multiplic-ity of motives we all carry within us.

Lost Psalm of King David
Sitting vigil with the heart's lust,
I am awakened again in the night with
hunger for touch and moan, to know
myself as a stalking, red-eyed lion.

Early steel blue blush brings generous vow
of threshold words. The hour of psalm-writing,
dedicated to the divine,
knowing myself as nightingale.

Late morning I wander to the cypress tree,
where my inner cacophony of voices
hatch murderous plans of victory,
rising like a Leviathan from the sea.

At sun's peak I dance with abandon
in front of the tabernacle, forgetting
myself for a moment, I become a gathering
of joy and bones on dappled grass.

Green silence of evening presses me
against my someday promise of death,
kindles a warrior's battle grip of anger,
fists held tight like stones, I am steed.

Dandelion seeds float and hover
in the dark like my mind drifting
into dreamscape, full of the majesty
of hawks, meandering through orchards.

I pluck the apple and see myself
in skin, flesh, seed, stem, and juice dripping.
I know myself as tesserae,
as weightlessness of cloud and heft of rock.

This is all of me, a set of tributaries
snaking out in a hundred directions.
Gather my fragments into Your great hands,
this jumble of caprice and impulse.

We know ourselves as sacred, blessed by the world.
We know ourselves as savage, fighting on too many fine mornings.
I no longer know what to cry out for,
I only know to write this prayer down for all to see.

May you embrace your sovereignty as the gift that you are to the world. May you see how claiming your own beauty and joy empowers others to do the same.

MY SOUL PROCLAIMS THE GREATNESS OF OUR GOD. MY SPIRIT REJOICES IN GOD.

MARY, MOTHER OF GOD

Mary: The Mother

Where does one begin with Mary? She appears throughout the gospels, most notably at the beginning and the end. She is the one who is asked to say yes to the holy birthing and surrender herself to something far beyond her imagining. She is the one who stands at the foot of the cross when her son is brutalized and murdered. She stays with him throughout the journey of suffering and into death. It is interesting to consider how much the scriptures focus on her presence at these thresholds of Jesus' life.

There is the Annunciation, when she is asked for consent, and the Visitation, when two cousins connect over their pregnancies and feel the intimacy of being in this space together. Mary's poem and song of justice, the Magnificat, has allusions to the Song of Hannah from the Hebrew scriptures, connecting her to a lineage of wise women. There are a couple of appearances during Jesus' lifetime, and then again she appears at the end of his life, standing witness at the foot of the cross with other women, when so many have run away. She was there at the Feast of Pentecost. In some traditions, she is this woman in the book of Revelation: "And a great portent appeared in heaven: A woman clothed with the sun, and the moon under her feet, and on her head a crown of twelve stars" (Rv 12:1).

Stories of Mary have been used in various ways to reinforce a certain image of womanhood. In the Christian tradition, which can lean so heavily on images of male sanctity and masculine divinity, Mary offers us another perspective. She is the embodiment of the sacred feminine, a window into another understanding of the divine presence. While our focus on her is the archetype of the Mother, she could also invite us to explore the archetype of the Virgin, which in older traditions had nothing to do with physical intactness, but everything to do with one who was whole unto her- or himself.

She has many titles, including Queen of Heaven. Mary has also been known as Our Lady of Sorrows, the one who can bear the tremendous weight of our grief. She is the one who knows aching loss and does not run away in the face of its fierceness. There are stories of the seven sorrows she had to bear. Joyce Rupp's beautiful book *Your Sorrow Is My Sorrow: Hope and Strength in Times of Suffering* invites readers to enter into Mary's sorrows and find themselves there, accompanied, and offered solace. There is a parallel tradition of Mary's seven joys. She is the container for our struggles and joys. She is the source of compassion. She is the birth mother and the death mother.

When my mother died in 2003, I felt the terrible loss of a mother presence in my life. Even though I embraced a spirituality that was less patriarchal and more feminine, it took the loss of my own mother to thrust me into the beginnings of a more profound relationship with the divine in her feminine form.

When John and I moved to Vienna in the summer of 2012, I had a series of experiences that led me deeper into the heart of Mary: the gift of an icon of Our Lady of Czestochowa, a potent night dream, an invitation to visit Mariazell ("Mary of the Cell," a Black Madonna in Austria), and a series of synchronicities that ultimately confirmed our move to Ireland all indicated to me that Mary was inviting me into her mysteries. What continues to unfold for me is a radical sense of Mary as that divine mother who calls us to a profound sense of rest, to the utter release of agendas, no more reaching or striving, just the simple gift of being in her presence and feeling embraced by compassion.

I realized for many years I resisted the sweet and pure image of her I saw so often in churches. I wanted to experience Mary as fierce as well, as the one who would stay present with me through all of the terrible things I had to witness and endure. I wanted Mary to be the keeper of boundaries, like a protective mother bear. I found this more powerful presence in her representation as the Black Madonna, whose darkness honors the mysteries of night wisdom, incubation, and gestation and who initiated me into the wider possibilities of Mary's gifts.

Mary was enormously significant for Hildegard of Bingen, whom we explore in chapter 11. Hildegard saw her as essential to the Incarnation, as the woman who said yes so that divinity could become flesh. In medieval monastic tradition, Mary played a central role, especially for the Cistercians and Bernard of Clairvaux (twelfth century) who had special devotion to her and emphasized her title as "Star of the Sea" (*Stella Maris*), the name of a star since ancient times that provided celestial navigation for sailors at night. Bernard writes, "If the winds of temptation arise; If you are driven upon the rocks of tribulation look to the star, call on Mary; If you are tossed upon the waves of pride, of ambition, of envy, of rivalry, look to the star, call on Mary. Should anger, or avarice, or fleshly desire violently assail the frail vessel of your soul, look at the star, call upon Mary." We may resist the night as a time when we feel lost, but that is the time when the star we can steer by appears.

Mary as Mother is the expression of infinite compassion and care. She is the experience of love that embraces us when we feel as if we may fall apart. One of my favorite books about Mary is David Richo's *Mary Within Us: A Jungian Contemplation of Her*

Titles and Powers: "All beings realize themselves in love which is a centralizing power that preserves us from fragmenting. . . . There is a loving intent in the universe that wants to exert itself in our choices and actions. The most beautiful of human challenges is to let that happen. The most powerful of divine promises is that it will happen."

We are invited to cooperate with this love and grace always available to us, to say yes to holy birthing, the way Mary herself did. Mary is, of course, just one face of this immense divine feminine presence in the world who goes by many names.

ICON SYMBOLISM: MARY

The quote on the icon, "my soul proclaims the greatness of our God, my spirit rejoices in God," comes from the Magnificat, her song of justice and tenderness.

This visual depiction of Mary is based on Our Lady of Czestochowa, whom I mentioned above, one of the Black Madonnas found in Poland. This is just one of dozens of different ways she has appeared as the dark feminine face of the divine.

The pear tree is from a personal encounter I had with Mary, where I saw her as the full ripe fruit-flesh of the pear, offering nourishment to me, bending toward me. I later discovered that Mary, and especially the Black Madonnas, are often depicted holding a pear in their hands.

She appears at night for she contains the wisdom of the dark, the cycles of the moon, and the rhythms of all creation.

Let your eyes rest on this image for a while and enter into a visual prayer with Mary as inspiration and guide.

THE ARCHETYPE OF THE MOTHER

The Mother, in the fullness of her form, is the source of all life and nourishment, of unconditional love and care, the generous flow of abundance and grace. We see this archetype alive in images of the divine as the Great Mother, whether Mother Nature, Gaia, or a goddess figure. She is the abundant provider of care and nurture. She is the face of compassion.

Each of us has a human mother, someone who physically gave birth to us. We first experience the mother in physical form in different ways. This might be the person who also loved and nurtured us or that role might belong to another. We may have been very close to our mothers or felt very distant. Our own mothers were limited by their own wounds—their unmet dreams and their times of abandonment projected onto us—which all emerge in our experience of the shadow Mother. These all impact our understanding of this archetype.

Both of these facets can sometimes make it challenging to access our inner Mothers. We have within us this ultimate source of compassion and care. We do not need to seek it in others. We have within us this immense source of grace and love.

I know when my own earthly mother died I entered a long period of profound grief. My journey has been to the Great Mother, reclaiming the divine feminine in my life in a deeper way, and ultimately reclaiming/recovering/restoring the Mother who dwells within me and offers me everything I need in terms of nourishment, affection, and attention. I began finding the Mother more keenly in forests and the sea, those places of wild belonging and connection to a sense of what is primal.

I personally experience this archetype primarily in a physical way. For me, she evokes a sense of generous abundance, of not needing to reach or strive for anything and seeing myself as perfectly *enough*.

The Mother is the one who supports us in giving birth to what is gestating within. She calls forth the power to birth and sustain life, whether a child or a creative vision. Sometimes through birth we are also called to experience a death of some kind, and the Mother accompanies us here as well. These are the times when the Mother is often activated, when we begin to discover our inner resources available through her. While the Mother is associated with the female gender, she is present in each of us, whether male or female.

THE SHADOW SIDE OF THE MOTHER

The wounds of our own mothers can be passed on to us. Often the shadow side of the Mother comes out in the martyr role, doing everything for others but never feeling appreciated or valued.

The Mother may project all her unmet needs on her children, asking them unconsciously to fulfill her in the ways she couldn't herself or to live out the dreams she never followed.

The shadow Mother can sacrifice her individuality or deny her children their individuality and own experiences in life. When the Mother demands that others meet her needs or she feels she has given up her identity, then she has entered the shadow realm.

- -

JESUS AND THE MOTHER ARCHETYPE: "LET THE CHILDREN COME TO ME"
REFLECTION BY JOHN VALTERS PAINTNER

Jerusalem, Jerusalem, the city that kills the prophets and stones those who are sent to it! How often have I desired to gather your children together as a hen gathers her brood under her wings, and you were not willing! See, your house is left to you, desolate. For I tell you, you will not see me again until you say, "Blessed is the one who comes in the name of the Lord."

—Matthew 23:37–39

Begin by reading the whole scripture passage as indicated and then pray with the excerpt in a contemplative way such as lectio divina (see guidelines in the appendix).

The preceding verses of this chapter in Matthew's gospel see Jesus condemning the scribes and Pharisees. He acknowledges that what they say is good and the people should *listen* to them. But Jesus then goes on to warn the people not to follow the example of the scribes and Pharisees.

Jesus points out that the religious leaders have raised themselves onto a high pedestal (the chair of Moses, no less), and look down on the people. They see the people as ones who should serve them. Jesus accuses the scribes and Pharisees of putting up barriers between the people and God, making themselves the gatekeepers.

Jesus is rejecting this model of false piety and spiritual exclusivity. When he says he yearns to gather the children together, it is a symbol of the right relationship between God and the people. In the Incarnation God came to walk among the people, to serve them. As a mother makes sacrifices and lovingly serves her children, so too does God yearn to protect and lift up the people.

Jesus is always maternal, ever the hen watching over the chicks or the shepherd seeking out the lost sheep. But perhaps no more so than when he calls the children to him, against the disciples' complaints, and blesses them.

Modern Western culture is changing. The role of men in child rearing is greater than ever. And yet, remnants of the old mentality still persist. Stay-at-home dads are rare and often mocked. Working mothers are sometimes vilified, damned if they do and damned if they don't. We need to break through these stereotypes so that all can embrace the inner archetypes.

Biology is only one aspect of motherhood. Whenever we nurture another, or even ourselves, to maturity and independence, we are like Jesus, calling the little ones to us.

THE PRACTICE OF STABILITY

In monastic tradition, stability is another of the great virtues. On a literal level, stability was the vow the monks made to stay with one community their whole lives. This was to avoid the practice of going from one monastery to another, always leaving when conflict arose or dissatisfaction entered in.

As the desert mothers and fathers knew, you carry yourself wherever you go. If you were to leave a place to avoid certain dynamics or relationship patterns, you would only discover them again in the next place you arrived at.

Beyond this layer, stability calls us to stay present to our commitments, to stay with our practice, and to value what happens when we wrestle with the discomfort that arises rather than run away through distraction. We may have begun this book with great intentions and slowly drifted from our practice. Stability calls us to gently return again and again.

Stability is the solid anchor that helps us to avoid falling into the shadow side of seeking in which we are always looking beyond the horizon for the next thing to save us, never savoring our current experience and recognizing the grace and sacredness already present.

We can spend a lot of time buying books about prayer and meditation without ever actually sitting down to the practice itself. This is the great paradox of the spiritual path: we are called to journey deeper into the Self to ultimately discover that what we seek we already have. Stability calls us to engage rather than only distantly ponder.

The Mother is the one who helps us to stay with everything that feels difficult or uncomfortable, and she reminds us when we want to run far away that right here and now that there is an abundance of love and compassion being offered, of the deep healing we dream about. She helps us to know the gifts that emerge when we stay with the unknowing, when we don't look away from what frightens or unsettles us. She is there with us right in the midst of things.

MEDITATION: INVITING YOUR INNER MOTHER

Begin to make the journey inward by slowing down your breath and settling into your body. Check in with your body and see if it needs anything, perhaps the softening of tight places or the ease of rest. Let your breath carry you gently to a place of peace, imagining that you are coming to rest in your center, bringing your awareness down to your heart. Dwell here for a few moments, letting yourself receive the divine compassion that exists within you.

Invite Mary to be present with you in this space of prayer. See how she wants to appear to you on this day. Rest there for a while in her presence, feeling the Spirit close as well.

Mary calls on you to awaken to your own inner Mother. She wants you to embrace that dimension of yourself that can offer as much love and nourishment as you need.

As your inner Mother arises, ask her to show you the births you have experienced, knowing these may appear as images or symbols. Spend some time savoring these. Notice what arises and allow it space.

Then ask her to show you the deaths that have been a part of your life as well, and honor those threshold experiences. Allow

the grief to visit you again, with the Mother as a conscious presence, a sacred container. Gently hold all those times when sorrow
wrapped itself around you.

Embark on this journey together and see what is revealed to
you. How have the births and deaths of life become thresholds of
initiation? What wisdom have they imparted to you? And where
did you experience the abiding power of compassion through the
dark nights and luminous days? You may not have the answers to
these questions, but the Mother invites you to sit with them as
mysteries, without trying to force or figure it out.

You might consider asking what is the new thing she is bringing to birth in you? And what must die to make way for this?
Know her presence as steady and sure, as generous and graced, as
you listen to her response.

Savor for a moment the Mother, Mary, and the Spirit with you,
committed to abide throughout whatever comes. See if a gesture
wants to arise in your hands or body to express the gifts of this
time of prayer.

When you feel ready to return to the room, gently allow your
breath to carry you back across the threshold of awareness. Spend
some time writing and reflecting on what insights emerged.

MANDALA EXPLORATION: GUSH ART MANDALAS

For this archetype, I invite you into an experience of gush art,
which means process-oriented drawing. You will need plain paper,
or you can do this in a journal.

Begin with some centering, which might involve moving into
silence, paying attention to your breath, becoming present to
your body, or just calling your awareness to the sacred presence
already with you.

Awaken your energy through gentle movement. Consider some
easy stretching, yoga poses, or putting on a piece of music and just

letting your body move how it longs to. This is a time to really notice what would feel good and nourishing. Movement will help to move your awareness down into your body, so you can release your thinking mind.

Sit down to your art journal or sheet of blank paper.

Decide whether music would support your process or if silence works better (part of what we're doing here is setting up conditions for you to notice how to trust and support yourself).

Draw a circle on the page either with a compass or with the bottom of a jar. As you draw this circle let it be an act of prayer. You are creating a mandala or sacred container for your art-making. Placing the circle on the page is an act of commitment to yourself, to creating this space within by which you can let whatever is moving through you come forth. You are creating the container—or tabernacle—for this time.

Connect again to your breath and invite the Spirit and your inner Mother to be active in this process. Begin to explore images and symbols through color and shape. With markers, colored pencils, or crayons, notice which colors are drawing you at this time without judgment or expectation. When thoughts such as "I always pick that color" or "I never pick that color" come to mind, be with them and see if you can return to your breath and let them go, returning only to the process. Explore how your inner Mother is moving you to create without judgment or trying to control the outcome.

Be fully aware of the process. Notice what thoughts or feelings arise. This is art as meditation, so we are cultivating our inner witness through this process. The witness is that calm, compassionate, curious, and infinitely wise part of ourselves that can observe what is happening internally without getting hooked by it. Remember that this isn't about making beautiful art but about being true to what is happening inside of you. We are cultivating the habit of not censoring ourselves, of noticing what is arising, letting it have space, and witnessing it.

Once you come to a place of completion with your piece, let yourself have a few moments of sitting in stillness. Let go of all thoughts and awareness for a brief time and just rest into a space of being rather than doing.

Then move into a time of brief journaling and reflection. Spend a few minutes writing about what you noticed in this experience: What inner voices did you encounter, what were the challenges and moments of ease? You are trying to not analyze your creation but to tend to the process, name what happened, and be curious about your experience.

FOR REFLECTION

- What about Mary's story most inspires or energizes you? Where do you feel the strongest connection or disconnection?
- What is your relationship to Mary of the scriptures? Has the Great Mother invited you into her embrace?
- What concrete steps toward mothering can you make in your life?
- How might you practice stability and this sense of being fully present to your experience?
- What did the visual art exploration experience reveal to you?

CLOSING BLESSING

The Annunciation and Nativity are archetypal stories, meaning that they invite us into our own personal annunciations and the birthings we are called to nurture. In a world that rushes through life, never pausing or resting, love can get squeezed out. We can forget what is of fundamental importance and feel cynical about the world. Mary and the Mother are reminders of the essential goodness of life. I love the image of Mary as keeper of the thresholds of birth and death, as the One who companions us on these transitions throughout our lives as we continuously give birth, as we die again and again.

There Is No Time for Love to Be Born

Aren't there annunciations
of one sort or another
in most lives?

—Denise Levertov

There is no time for love to be born
in a world flailing under fear,
trampled by terror, crushed by callousness.
There is no room for love to be born
under the heft of pressing grief,
no open portals in the perpetual busyness
or the list of endless tasks minted newly each morning,
where "to do" never seems to include "love more."
No opening in the jostled and tinseled shops,
which promise to soothe the ache and awfulness of our burdens.

I see you there holding your infant son, pink-scrubbed and new.
I see you there holding his grown dead body, brutalized and hollow.
Your sobs rumble protest as he is lifted from your arms,
longing to still be earth-tethered by the weight of blood and bones.
You are not orbiting the sun,
but instead the great dirge, swaying me from note to note,
the wailing daughter whose mother's heartbeat has just halted,
the river's cold splash when another one gives up,
the soldier's wound that sends him home,
the slivered crescent descending against a black horizon,
the winter's pale morning light streaming between dusty curtains,
the newly discovered constellation.
You are the birth mother and the death mother.

There is no time for love to be born,
only the willing descent into all the battered and frozen places,
the opening of doors long ago latched and rusted.

Comets slash the sky with warnings of direness.
You are the breaking open of star-streaked
cracks where woe loses its sturdy grip,
where in the most ordinary of moments,
when all else nudges us further toward despair,

suddenly we feel the wild impulse arising
to say yes.

May you be blessed with a yes on your lips and in your heart to the holy invitations that come your way. May you find yourself in intimate partnership at all of the times of birth you are called to labor through, and may you know yourself held through a thousand losses and times of grief. May the Mother nourish you with lavish generosity.

Dorothy Day: The Orphan

• •

INTRODUCTION TO DOROTHY DAY

Dorothy Day (1897–1980) was born in New York state on November 8, 1897. As a child, she took an early interest in religion and converted to Catholicism as an adult.

When she was a young college student, Dorothy was interested in social activism. She became more active in social justice and worked for several publications dedicated to a variety of causes.

She was a very human figure who had an abortion when she was younger and then a daughter, Tamar, born out of wedlock, whom she raised as a single mother and loved dearly. When she converted to Catholicism it caused tremendous friction with the father of her child who wanted nothing to do with religion. This conversion was a decisive turning point in her life.

We are fortunate that she had a great love of writing, so we are able to have an intimate experience of her daily observations and reflections. In her autobiography, *The Long Loneliness*, she described her early habit of keeping a diary: "When I was a child, my sister and I kept notebooks; recording happiness made it last longer, we felt, and recording sorrow dramatized it and took away its bitterness; and often we settled some problem which beset us, even while we wrote about it." She maintained this habit throughout her life so that we have large collections of her diary entries illuminating some of her response to life. Sadly the diaries from her very early life are lost, but we have a large collection to draw upon to understand her more mature thinking.

She later befriended Peter Maurin who wanted to spread the radical message of the gospels. Together they started the newspaper called *The Catholic Worker* in the 1930s. The newspaper, along with the movement of the same name, has grown into a leading voice for the poor and against injustice.

In an editorial, she described the mission of *The Catholic Worker*: "For those who are sitting on park benches in the warm spring sunlight. For those who are huddling in shelters trying to escape the rain. For those who are walking the streets in the all but futile search for work. For those who think that there is no hope for the future, no recognition of their plight—this little paper is addressed."

She would describe the writing of her regular column as a letter to friends and "an act of community," a reaching out to others who shared the same values and principles. She eventually called her column "On Pilgrimage" to reflect her sense of always journeying.

Dorothy Day was very much committed to those who were "outcasts" and on the fringes of society. She loved the widow and the orphan. She was passionate about the corporal works of mercy: feeding the hungry, sheltering those without homes, and providing clothes for the naked. She was always trying to see Christ in "the poor lost ones, the abandoned ones, the sick, the crazed, the solitary human beings whom Christ so loved, in whom I see, with a terrible anguish, the body of this death."

Soon after the newspaper began, Peter and Dorothy opened a soup kitchen and homeless shelter, and Peter challenged bishops to open "houses of hospitality" in every diocese, to live out the message of the Gospel. As the number of houses grew, they were open to everyone. Dorothy resisted creating a formal rule of life; she saw it as more of a family, often with the chaos that comes from many people in great need living together.

Dorothy also demonstrated against war, stood in picket lines with United Farmworkers Union, and challenged the IRS over taxes and registering as a nonprofit.

To sustain herself, she attended daily Mass and prayed the monastic Hours. She was also a Benedictine Oblate at St. Procopius Abbey in Lisle, Illinois, and often went there on retreat. Dorothy's spirituality was very earthy, finding the sacred in the most ordinary of moments and encounters. She saw the sacraments as sustaining her in this life she chose so freely. Her faith was rooted in reaching out to the needs of others, and she was sustained by regular prayer and worship. Yet she often came into conflict with the Church over her activities.

Dorothy's favorite saint was Thérèse of Lisieux, the "Little Flower," who died the same year Dorothy was born. Dorothy was very drawn to Thérèse's "little way" of infusing all daily activities with a prayerful awareness and intention as well as a spirit of love. She loved the phrase "duty of delight," which comes from nineteenth-century critic John Ruskin. She repeated it often as a reminder to herself to find beauty in the midst of every moment.

Dorothy encountered many struggles in her life of illness, financial woes, community friction, and the struggles that come from poverty such as lice, bed bugs, outbreaks of violence, noise, foul smells, constant anxiety over support, loneliness, and more.

She also found much joy in her daughter and grandchildren, as well as in times away on retreat or at the beach, listening to music, reading the scriptures, and in prayer.

Dorothy Day died on November 29, 1980. Although she famously said, "*Don't* call me a *saint. I don't want* to be *dismissed* so
easily," the Church has begun the canonization process.

ICON SYMBOLISM: DOROTHY DAY

The quote above the icon comes from Dorothy Day: "Heaven is a
banquet and life is a banquet, too." This reflects her incarnational
spirituality. As someone who spent a large part of her time with
those who were homeless and hungry, she had a unique perspective on the banquet of life.

She is shown holding a soup ladle to represent the meals she
offered to those who were in need and a diamond ring, which
someone gave to her and she ended up giving to a homeless woman as Dorothy had no need for such things. She appreciated the
dignity this act brought.

The scene is an urban one, with a stray cat and pigeons as her
companions.

I invite you to spend some time with Dorothy Day in this image and see how your prayer unfolds in response.

THE ARCHETYPE OF THE ORPHAN

The Orphan appears across myths, fairy tales, and popular culture. Think of Little Orphan Annie, Cinderella, Dorothy in the
Wizard of Oz, and Harry Potter. The Genesis story of the Garden
of Eden is a primal orphan myth explaining how our experience
of being exiles arises. Jesus experiences utter abandonment on the
Cross.

The fundamental experience of the Orphan is abandonment,
feeling like an exile, and longing for an experience of being at
home. The Orphan archetype in each of us is activated by all the
experiences in which the child in us feels abandoned, betrayed,
victimized, neglected, or disillusioned. We are all orphaned in

one way or another simply because we are raised by parents with their own wounds and, somewhere along the way, they have orphaned us—we each have an inner Orphan.

While our first instinct may be to run when our inner feelings of need and loneliness arise, the central task of the Orphan is to feel this pain of being an unmothered child. Ideally we do this hard work from a place of strength and feeling good rather than waiting until we feel awful. We are invited to face our experiences of pain and disillusionment. The Orphan calls us to wake up, let go of our illusions, and face painful realities. We all have losses and catastrophes; we all carry grief that has gone unmourned, that has been pushed away.

The Orphan can also help to crack open our intuition and empathy. Those who suffer much in conscious ways are often able to offer that as a gift back to the community. The Orphan also invites us into an interdependence with others as we realize that we are all wounded in some way.

Ultimately, the Orphan learns that it is the source of power to face one's victimization and limitations and to feel fully the pain caused by them. Conscious suffering is the gateway to our own spiritual awakening and maturity. Doing so frees us up to work together to create a better world. The healing begins when we really feel the pain and reality of our orphaning experiences, and it progresses when we recognize how we have denied part of ourselves. The gift of the Orphan is to connect to our own wounding, to find safe spaces to share it and to bond, and to create relationships of mutual love and care.

THE SHADOW SIDE OF THE ORPHAN

To the degree that we do not acknowledge the Orphan inside us, that Orphan is abandoned by us as well as the world. We can perpetuate this cycle of abandonment in many ways. Sometimes we are so afraid of being left by someone that we leave before they have a chance, so we never allow ourselves the possibility of healing. The Orphan may do something to provoke rejection simply to have a greater sense of control over life. Since disappointment, rejection, and abandonment are seen as inevitable, we feel just a bit better by leaving first (self-betrayal and abandonment).

Originally betrayed by others, Orphans often betray their own hopes and dreams because they expect disappointment. Ironically, the more we live false, inauthentic lives in order to be safe from hurt, the more orphaned, hurt, and disillusioned we become. We have essentially turned against ourselves.

Another shadow is cynicism about the world that leads us to a sense of powerlessness as we allow ourselves to give up on any action for good.

JESUS AND THE ORPHAN ARCHETYPE: "MY GOD, WHY HAVE YOU ABANDONED ME?"
REFLECTION BY JOHN VALTERS PAINTNER

When it was noon, darkness came over the whole land until three in the afternoon. At three o'clock Jesus cried out with a loud voice, "Eloi, Eloi, lema sabachthani?" which means, "My God, my God, why have you forsaken me?"

—Mark 15:33–34

Begin by reading the whole scripture passage as indicated and then pray with the excerpt in a contemplative way such as lectio divina (see guidelines in the appendix).

It is difficult to think of the Second Person of the Holy Trinity as being orphaned or feeling abandoned. And yet, at that moment on the Cross, how could he not?

To reach this point in the gospels, nailed to a tree and dying, Jesus has been betrayed by one of his closest disciples and abandoned by the rest. He has been slandered, mocked, beaten, and now executed in the slowest and most painful way, all in full view of his detractors who gloat at his utter undoing. The only surprising thing about Jesus crying out, "My God, my God, why have you forsaken me?" is that he had the strength left to say anything.

But why these words? What was Jesus trying to impart with his dying breath?

Originally, the psalms were not numbered as we have them today. And they did not have titles, as such. But our spiritual ancestors would memorize them and know them by the first verse, the way some modern poems are today. And so one could merely recite this first line and others from the community would call to mind the rest of the psalm, like one might make a point about the dangers of lying by simply mentioning "the boy who cried wolf." Collectively, we all remember the story from childhood and are reminded of the moral.

Some have suggested that this is what Jesus was doing on the Cross. He did not have the strength to recite the entire psalm, so he speaks the first line. Those who heard it would know the full psalm, including the fact that after an opening expressing the author's feeling of total abandonment, the psalm ends with reassurances of God's faithfulness.

One might think this means Jesus really didn't feel orphaned in that moment as the psalm ends on an upbeat note. But that would be missing something very important. Jesus was indeed in a very dark place. He felt, if even for a moment, the heart of the Orphan. The psalm he chose to invoke does begin in a very dark place. It is a place we can all relate to, no matter how large our family or circle of friends. Even if momentarily, Jesus felt the loss and loneliness of being alone in the world.

THE PRACTICE OF HOSPITALITY

All guests who present themselves are to be welcomed as Christ, for he himself
will say: I was a stranger and you welcomed me.

—Rule *of Benedict, 53*

I find hospitality to be one of the most significant and most challenging of all the monastic virtues. The core of this idea was that everyone who comes to the door of the monastery, and by extension the door of our lives—the poor, the traveler, those of a different religion, social class, or education—should be welcomed in, not just as an honored guest but as a revelation of the sacred. For Benedict, our encounter with the stranger, the unknown, the unexpected, and the foreign elements that spark our fear are precisely the places where we are most likely to encounter God. This is a practice of *outer* hospitality.

Monastic spirituality calls us to see everything and everyone, including ourselves, as holy. The places in our heart where we struggle or resist are to be embraced with kindness. The person who irritates us or makes us feel fearful is a window into how God is at work in our lives.

There is another dimension to this practice that we sometimes might be tempted to forget, which is *inner* hospitality. Within each of us we have a multitude of feelings, experiences, and inner selves that we would prefer to close the door on. We have many inner strangers knocking at the door of our hearts. How many times have I refused to welcome grief or anger, the scary new dream, the embarrassing aspect I want to deny, or the part of myself that doesn't seem to fit with the others?

We each contain a Self that is the true heart of who we are beneath all of the roles and identities we play. It is sometimes called the inner witness, and it is that place within us that can calmly observe what happens within us and can be with the thoughts that come up and the stories we tell ourselves. The witness brings curiosity and compassion. In religious traditions, the mystics tell us this is the place where we encounter the divine within.

The early desert monks would say, "Go, sit in your cell, and your cell will teach you everything." The cell is both an internal and external place. We carry our monastic cell with us everywhere we go. It is a symbol for the place within our hearts where we wrestle with our inner struggles and encounter God's presence in the midst of the wrestling.

In the desert tradition, when we enter the cave of our heart we encounter the passions that might also be described as habits of being that developed from a core wound, often from childhood. These wounds distort the reality of who we are and lead us to compulsive acts. They need to be tended and healed, which is challenging because they connect us to our deepest vulnerability. In one strand of the desert tradition, passions were viewed as something negative, to be eradicated from the soul, and we sometimes read about the language of doing battle with them.

However, the dominant teaching from the desert mothers and fathers was that the passions were considered something positive—natural and neutral impulses whose source is God—but in our human efforts to suppress them, their energy becomes misdirected. Some of the language used is "knowing the passions," where *knowing* means loving and embracing. The goal is to illumine them, rather than eliminate them; we seek to not destroy them but channel them.

One of the desert fathers, Abba Isaiah, claims that all of the passions including anger, jealousy, and lust are given to us by God with a particular and sacred purpose. Coming to know these passions, how they were formed, and what they desire is a healing experience. We begin to reclaim all the parts of ourselves in the service of wholeness.

This practice of inner hospitality means welcoming in whatever it is we are experiencing as having the possibility of wisdom for us. The Orphan knows the power of tenderness and vulnerability and just wants to be seen rather than fixed. Hospitality is a lifetime journey; we don't one day figure it out and no longer have to struggle with our impulses and desires. But we can learn not to resist them and instead find ways to enter into dialogue with them so we can deepen and grow into spiritual maturity.

MEDITATION: INVITING YOUR INNER ORPHAN

Begin by creating a safe and sacred space for yourself. It is especially important for this time to be free from interruptions or intrusions from others. Connect to your breath and allow the rhythm of inhale and exhale to draw you deeper. Just become aware of what you are feeling right now, and see if you can be with it without trying to change anything. Notice any commentary on your experience and simply let it go, allowing you to feel how you are.

Invite in the presence of Dorothy Day, welcome her and notice how she wants to appear to you. Welcome in the Spirit, and ask both of them to help reveal to you your inner Orphan. Be open to receiving images that may come or symbols that may arise. Pay attention to body sensations or other feelings. Connect with this tender part of yourself that has experienced abandonment or any sort of loneliness, isolation, or rejection.

As emotions arise, welcome each one. Breathe into them without holding on tightly to any of them; just notice them rise and fall.

Let your Orphan know that you, along with Dorothy Day and the Spirit, are here to witness your experience and to see this part of yourself with immense compassion.

Listen for what she or he asks of you. See if a gift is offered. Move this into your body, and hold a gesture that expresses this invitation or gift. Connect to your breath again and then return to the room, writing down anything that you would like to honor with words.

MANDALA EXPLORATION: GUSH ART MANDALAS

You are invited again to move into mandala-making through the medium of gush art. Gather your colored drawing materials and a blank piece of paper. Begin by breathing gently and allowing some movement to awaken your body. A powerful song for meditation is the old gospel classic "Sometimes I Feel Like a Motherless Child"; you might search online to see if you can find a recording to listen to.

Listen for the grace you desire in this time of prayer. Allow the colors to choose you as you begin putting marks to paper. Start by drawing with intention the circle that contains the mandala.

Then follow the impulse of your Orphan in putting down color, shape, and symbol. Allow yourself ten to fifteen minutes or whenever you feel completed. Be with this image with loving compassion, breathing in its gifts. When you are ready you can write about the process and dialogue with the images and colors.

WRITING EXPLORATION: FAIRY TALE

The fairy tale is a lovely way to honor the Orphan, since she or he often appears in stories of this nature. There are a couple of ways you might approach this. The first is to simply write the words "Once upon a time" and then follow the story where it leads. You can draw upon the voices from the mandala exploration.

For a more structured story form, you can try using the one below.[1] After each prompt, allow yourself a few minutes to write something to fill it in, and then continue to the next one:

- Once upon a time . . .
- And every day . . .
- Until one day . . .
- Because of this . . .
- Until finally . . .
- And ever since that day . . .

FOR REFLECTION
- What about Dorothy Day's story most inspires or energizes you? Where do you feel the strongest connection or disconnection?
- How do you sabotage your own dreams because of fear of abandonment?
- How have your orphaning experiences been rites of passage, initiating you into a deeper wisdom?
- How might you practice hospitality and this sense of welcoming in all of the tender and wounded places within you?
- What did the visual art exploration experience reveal to you?

CLOSING BLESSING
After Dorothy Day wrote her autobiography, *The Long Loneliness*, she later wrote that she thought her next autobiographical work should be called "The Duty of Delight," after a favorite quote by John Ruskin. It was the title given to a collection of her diaries published posthumously. Even with long days spent meeting the needs of those who were homeless and hungry and fighting against the horrors of war, she found her greatest solace in beauty. Cultivating joy became essential to her to sustain her vision. This poem arises out of this conviction.

The Duty of Delight
After Dorothy Day

This poem is held together by heartache,
by the sour smell of sorrow hovering,
thick dust and thinned soup,
the old pillowcase keening-damp,
the swift armada of black clouds.

Even while I write this,
bodies are burned alive in cages,
put on view for the world to see,
bodies are piled in unmarked pits,
or broken from a terrible hunger.

How to remember even the possibility of delight
late one evening after hours of bagging groceries,
the baby crying now, electricity shuts off.
Someone, somewhere, is shredded
and scattered by secret wounds.

Perhaps this is life's most exalted and exacting task,
holding the hard edges against the soft wonder,
or seeking the consolation of nature's indifference.
Even the flame turns to ash,
even the ash is fodder for roses.

What can I do but gather constellations into my arms
like sprays of Queen Anne's Lace?
What can I do but track a creature untamed,
deep into the thick forest?
What can I do but slip open the rusty, lichened gate?

What can I do but read poems before breakfast,
and allow my walking to become a fanfare?
My heart beats like a frog on a hot August night,
while the river rushes past like a herd of wild horses,
and I fall off the ragged edges of the map of known things.

This poem is held together by joy,
even when standing still
we are always rushing east toward the night,
hopeful to meet the sun again soon
soaring in pink perfection.

May you welcome in the tenderness and abandoned parts of yourself and discover there beauty and gift.

WE MUST KINDLE THE DIVINE FIRE IN OURSELVES

AMMA SYNCLETICA

Amma Syncletica: The Warrior

. . . .

INTRODUCTION TO
AMMA SYNCLETICA AND THE DESERT MOTHERS

Fortunately, the marvelous collection of sayings entitled *Sayings of the Desert Fathers* also includes several stories of the desert mothers, and there is another small collection of stories about female desert elders.

Generally, women in the early centuries of Christianity did not have control of their own lives or even their bodies. They were at the disposal of other people, normally other men, who owned them.

In the third- to sixth-century desert of Egypt, Syria, Palestine, and Arabia, a powerful movement happened. Christian monasticism began flowering in response to a call to leave behind the world. The center of this movement was in Egypt, and by the year AD 400, it was a land of monks experimenting with a variety of forms of monasticism, including the solitary life of the hermit and the communal form of monasticism. These spiritual seekers who came to be known as the desert fathers and mothers withdrew from a society where the misuse of human relationships, power, and material possessions ran counter to their sense of the sacredness of life.

Their journey into the desert was a movement toward cultivating an intentional awareness of God's presence and recognizing that worldly pleasures bring little long-term satisfaction. The aim was to experience God in each moment and activity by reducing their physical needs and committing themselves to the discipline of regular prayer and self-inquiry. This was the foundation of the monastic movement that flourished over the centuries that followed and still calls to us today.

By making the arduous journey into the desert, women were able to reject the patriarchal constraints and restrictions and find a life-giving alternative. In the desert, the *ammas* (mothers) were able to live with the same single focus as the *abbas* (fathers)—growing in intimacy with the divine presence.

These women were as fierce in their spiritual wisdom as their male counterparts. The titles of spiritual father or mother were given to them not because they played any kind of nurturing role but because they were considered to be wise elders steeped in years of desert experience.

When these women decided to leave their conventional lives behind—and many of them were well educated; some were quite wealthy, while some were prostitutes—they each made an intentional choice to live in a way alternate to the dominant culture. The ammas reveal that from the very beginnings of the life of the Church, women have been initiators of new patterns and teachings.

Amma Syncletica (380–460) is one of the three women who appeared in the *Sayings*. She was born in Alexandria in a wealthy family and was very well educated. When her parents died she sold everything and gave the money to the poor. She went with her blind sister to live as a hermit. Eventually a community of women formed around her, and she died in 460. We have twenty-seven of her sayings in the alphabetical collection.

One of the traditions of the desert was to seek a "word." We find this phrase often in the stories and sayings: *"give me a word,"* a seeker would ask an elder. The word they were seeking was often a phrase or image they could chew on for days or weeks, some wisdom to work on in their souls.

Here is one of her sayings:

> Amma Syncletica said, "In the beginning there are a great many battles and a good deal of suffering for those who are advancing towards God and afterwards, ineffable joy. It is like those who wish to light a fire; at first they are choked by smoke and cry, and by this means obtain what they seek (and it is said: 'Our God is a consuming fire' [Heb 12:24]), so we also must kindle the divine fire in ourselves through tears and hard work."[1]

Amma Syncletica counsels courage and hard work in this "battle." I have trouble with the metaphor of battles for the spiritual life that the desert elders often use. I resist that kind of violent imagery. And yet, in Benedictine monk and scholar Michael Casey's book on humility, he writes that "a much more creative way of dealing with difficult texts is to take our negative reaction as an indication that there may be an issue beneath the surface with which we must deal." When I experience resistance to what I am reading, I need to pay attention to what is being stirred within me.

There were two primary attitudes toward the passions in the desert. One was to consider them something to be eradicated. This is where the battle metaphor plays a significant role. The lifelong struggle is to eliminate them from our experience, and in this view, they are considered disordered and ultimately from the devil.

Demons play a large role in desert theology. In Evagrius's *Praktikos*, more than two-thirds of his writing discusses the nature of demons. What he calls the eight thoughts are considered to be demons at work with which he says every monk must do battle: gluttony, lust, anger, avarice, sadness, acedia, vainglory, and pride. This does not mean he thought of demons as purely psychological realities. According to William Harmless, Evagrius and the other desert ascetics believed in the reality of demons whose most common method of warfare with the desert dwellers was through their thoughts. He recommended that monks engage in watchfulness to observe the intensity of their thoughts, watching them rise and fall. Wisdom is won only by battle.

These passions, as they are also called, are much more than sins or vices, however. They are our inner wounds, calling us to embrace our vulnerability and brokenness—this is the desert path toward healing and wholeness—through being honest about that with which we struggle. Our shadow selves, those tender, hurting parts that are repressed in our psyches, are a part of the passions.

Passions are what Alan Jones says in his book *Soul Making: The Desert Way of Spirituality* are the "shifting, unfree, unintegrated part of ourselves."[2] These "impure thoughts" are also referred to by the term *logismoi*. The desert monks were seeking *hesychia*, a kind of deep inner stillness. Not just quiet but a profound sense of calm and trust. Upon going into the desert to free oneself of the responsibilities of daily life and seek the peace of hesychia, one was also stepping into a space where one could come face to face with these thoughts. In the solitude, monks had to face the daily assaults of discouragement and lethargy in spiritual practice and life, as well as the force of anger or lust. Of course, we encounter these as well in our lives. Our experience of these inner forces often feels like a wilderness place. This is where the metaphor of desert as an interior reality becomes especially important.

Amma Syncletica's story reinforces the need to stay with one's thoughts in fierce and patient battle. Staying with ourselves and our experience is the only way through.

We might also remember that battle is an archetypal idea, with the Warrior as an ancient expression of the one who goes to battle. This is an energy we all carry within us to varying degrees and that calls us to be fierce protectors of our boundaries. The Warrior in each of us is able to say yes and no very clearly. The desert elders lived in a fierce landscape that reminded them again and again to strip away the nonessentials. This is always a painful process and very hard work.

ICON SYMBOLISM: AMMA SYNCLETICA

The quote on the icon, "we must kindle the divine fire in ourselves," is from the first story I shared from Amma Syncletica. She is depicted dancing out in the Egyptian desert under the heat of the sun, accompanied by desert creatures like snakes and scorpions. In the background is the cave she would have used as her hermitage space, her monastic cell.

Sit with Amma's image for a while, imagining yourself there with her in the desert, and listen for the wisdom she has to offer you.

THE ARCHETYPE OF THE WARRIOR

The Warrior archetype is that part of ourselves which is ready to protect and defend whatever is necessary. We find this archetype often in great legends and films. The Warrior is depicted as strong, often invincible, loyal to the sovereign, willing to fight to the death for what is most valuable, and aligned with a just cause. While they are often depicted as men, women are just as likely to have this energy.

I also experience the Warrior as that part of myself able to create and maintain strong boundaries in my life, whether physical
or energetic. I draw on the Warrior to help me protect what I
claim as important. As a monk in the world, it is so easy at times
to let my contemplative practice go when life becomes too busy
and full. My Warrior is an ally, reminding me that I need to be
fierce at times to keep my own needs met.

As we see in the stories of the desert mothers and fathers, the
Warrior can also be drawn on for internal battles and to claim a
fierceness over what we will let into our own psychic space. These
are ancient practices for keeping ourselves whole. This is a form
of the Spiritual Warrior, one who goes to battle in another way.

Some of us who feel invested in nonviolence may be especially
resistant to claiming the inner Warrior, and yet this is a particularly important energy to be drawn upon in healthy ways. We all
have the need to set clear boundaries for ourselves, and fierceness
is called for in many situations. We all have times when we need
to protect something precious in our lives.

Richard Rohr describes the "sacred yes" and the "sacred no."
The sacred yes reflects the feminine archetype of welcoming, nurturing, enfolding energy—all those things, people, and opportunities we embrace.[3] The Orphan asks for this welcome. The
sacred no reflects the masculine archetype of boundary setting
and protection. We all have both these dimensions within us,
although likely one will be more developed than the other. Integration is about drawing on them in balance. The sacred no is the
healthy setting of limits and protection of our gifts and energies
so we don't over-extend ourselves. Sometimes our lives may be
filled with exuberant yeses, but an overabundance of good things
can be just as destructive to our energy and commitment when
we start to feel too stretched, when we lose focus on the deepest

thing calling us. Sometimes fierceness is necessary in keeping out what is not necessary or what may be harmful or poisonous.

SHADOW SIDE OF THE WARRIOR

One of the shadow sides of the Warrior is when we direct this fierceness at ourselves and work at subtly (and sometimes not so subtly) undermining our own efforts or the destruction of our desires. This comes out in our encounters with the inner critic, who can be fierce in its own way. Sometimes we need to meet this inner fierceness of the critic with the inner fierceness of the true Warrior. While I often counsel people to meet their critical voices with a sense of compassion and openness, sometimes after we listen to their stories, we also need to take the stance of the Warrior and say a strong and sacred no to them.

Another shadow side is the tyrant or terrorist who stops at nothing to get what they need, perpetrating violence on others to meet one's own needs. When the Warrior is not balanced with compassionate energy it can become overly aggressive and indiscriminately violent. The shadow Warrior distorts or abandons ethical principles in search of victory at any cost. We see this shadow side active across the globe, reported on daily in the news.

• •

JESUS AND THE WARRIOR ARCHETYPE: THE MONEYCHANGERS IN THE TEMPLE
REFLECTION BY JOHN VALTERS PAINTNER

Then he entered the temple and began to drive out those who were selling things there, and he said, "It is written, 'My house shall be a house of prayer, but you have made it a den of robbers.'" And every day he was teaching in the temple. The chief priests, the scribes, and the leaders of the people kept looking for a way

to kill him, but they did not find anything they could do, for all the people were
spellbound by what they heard.

—Luke 19:45–48

Begin by reading the whole scripture passage as indicated and then pray
with the excerpt in a contemplative way such as lectio divina (see guide-
lines in the appendix).

Many like to point out a perceived difference between the
wrathful God of the Old Testament and the peacefulness of Jesus in the gospels. But there are many examples of God's gentle
nature throughout the Hebrew scriptures. And then there is this
incident: Jesus fashioning a weapon and committing an act of
violence in the holiest of places in his own culture and religion.

The Temple was the center of Jewish faith and culture for
thousands of years. Its reconstruction after the Babylonian exile
was a catalyst for writing parts of the Bible. The rebuilding of
the Temple was an important symbol of the rebuilding of Jewish
identity and faith. There is much space devoted to the Temple in
the Hebrew scriptures: how and of what it is to be built; what will
be placed inside of it and for what purpose; and who is allowed
in and what they are allowed to do there. Spiritual purity is a recurring motif. One of these purity regulations specifies that only
certain animals, and of a particular condition, could be used in
the sacrificial ceremonies in the Temple. This was an issue in the
time of Jesus as most Jews were poor due to years of occupation.
This necessitated the buying of these "clean animals" at the outer
courtyard of the larger Temple complex. This purchase was further complicated by the need to purchase the animal with Jewish
coins, as Roman coins were seen as idolatrous.

These two religious hurdles (exchanging the common Roman
coins for the Temple currency and "the seller's market" of the
right type of animals) led to the situation at the heart of Jesus' response. The people, earnest in their desire to perform the required

sacrifices correctly, are first taken advantage of in the exchange of currency and then in the exorbitant prices for the animals. And all of this is done with the complete approval of the chief priests themselves.

What other course of action could Jesus have taken to make his point? The Romans didn't care about the internal religious affairs of a minor sect within their vast empire, the money changers and merchants were making too much money to want to change, and the religious authority used all this to retain control over the people. Words, alone, would have done nothing. Only the oppressed, those abused by the system and yet too powerless to fix it, would have heard them.

Being loving and peaceful does not mean one does not fight for what is right and just. People of good faith may argue over what is the most effective course of action, but there is no question that something must be done.

There is an important line between anger and righteous anger. Anger, on its own, can lead to hatred and destructive violence. Righteous anger is a motivator that is directed and purposeful, not a means to itself. Jesus is trying not to punish individuals but to draw attention to a corrupt system in need of change.

THE PRACTICE OF
"DOING BATTLE" WITH THOUGHTS
This practice is twofold. We must honor our feelings and we must acknowledge our thoughts.

First is the absolute importance of honoring how you feel. Consider the foundational premise of this book: that we are each made up of multiple inner energies or selves. These energies long to be welcomed in, in a radical act of inner hospitality. When I feel grief, I allow her in with tenderness. When I feel lonely, I welcome her to my inner table. When I feel unbridled joy, I let her have room to dance.

We aren't ever really taught how to be with ourselves and the different feeling-states that arise. Even after years of practice, I sometimes feel grief or loneliness and still want to push it away. I would rather not experience these things. And yet a shift happens when I allow myself to soften and welcome these parts in; when I can be tender with myself and honor my experience, I often experience those feelings losing their charge and intensity. They just want to have space.

Second is recognizing that attached to these feelings are thoughts and stories we tell ourselves about the feelings. Not all stories are helpful or life-giving. When an uncomfortable feeling such as grief, loneliness, anger, or even sometimes joy arises, we often have a set of thoughts attached to that feeling or a story we have created. This goes something like, "Oh God, I am feeling grief and sadness arise again; I thought I had gotten over that loss. What is wrong with me? Why can't I just be happy about what I have in my life?" Or when fear sets in about the changes you are feeling called to, the voice might be more of the inner critic or judge saying something like, "Who do you think you are? Why would you walk away from security? Why do you think you deserve something different?" You probably have your own version of these stories that arise, and different feelings probably bring up different narratives.

Your invitation is to pay attention to both feelings and thoughts. See if you can welcome in whatever your felt experience is, breathing into it, making room inside of you to welcome it in as part of the landscape of who you are in this moment.

When the undermining thoughts and stories, or the voices of the inner critic and judge, come up, notice them, and then as best you can, don't let them take root. Try not to follow their trail that always leads to discouragement and self-doubt. These voices are often anxious, nervous chatter, making declarations without nuance, offering nothing helpful, and seeing no alternatives. These voices try to sabotage us in many subtle ways.

In the desert tradition, this was referred to as "doing battle with one's thoughts." The "battle" imagery may or may not be helpful for you. I used to resist it until I recognized that we all have an inner Warrior whose work is to protect us from threats, both inner and outer. And it often does feel like a long and tiring battle with these thoughts that do not relent. When I called upon my inner Warrior, I found her fierce and strong presence very helpful. But find your own language around this. Don't let the metaphors limit your efforts.

This doesn't mean that all critical thinking is bad. Sometimes thoughts will come up that are more about being grounded in real circumstances, presenting/prompting a voice that comes in service to you without emotional charge and offers guidance and curiosity about the possibilities.

MEDITATION: INVITING YOUR INNER WARRIOR

Find a comfortable seated position, and begin by drawing in your breath long and slow and then exhaling long and slow in a gentle rhythm so you find yourself beginning to arrive in this moment. Notice how your body feels and if anything needs to shift to create more ease.

After a few moments of breath work, draw your awareness from your head down to your heart center. Notice what you are feeling right in this moment and practice being with it, without trying to change it.

In this place of heart-centered awareness invite in the presence of Amma Syncletica as a wise warrior woman. Notice how she is dressed and how she carries herself.

See Amma Syncletica invite in the presence of the Spirit and then together let them draw forth your own inner Warrior. Allow some time for this to unfold, noticing what kind of presence emerges from this imagining. Is your inner Warrior male or female? Does she or he carry any tools for the battle?

Then dropping more deeply inward, ask to be shown a place in your life where you are in need of stronger boundaries, a healthy and compassionate fierceness that allows you to say no when necessary. Ask for the wisdom of Amma Syncletica, the Spirit, and your inner Warrior in how to be with this situation. What is the grace needed? What wisdom do they have to offer?

After some time spent pondering this invitation, ask for a gift to help you to navigate the battles ahead. Bring this gift into your body through a gesture you can repeat later to remind yourself and to draw on the strength.

When you are ready, allow your breath to bring you back to the room and spend some time writing any insights received.

MANDALA EXPLORATION: COLLAGE MANDALAS

We move into working with collage in this chapter, so you will need images from magazines, catalogs, or even old art books. You will also need a circle cut out of paper or something heavier such as cardboard. You can also use a cake-round sold in baking supply stores or ask a local pizza restaurant if they will give you one of their unused cardboard rounds. I recommend about twelve inches in diameter. Have a glue stick and some scissors as well.

Gather all of your supplies and then find a time and space for your creative process. Begin with some movement to awaken your body's energy. Then connect with your breath and offer up a prayer or grace you seek for this time of creation. Welcome your inner Warrior to be a part of this experience.

As you begin sorting through images, notice which ones resonate with you and which ones create a sense of dissonance. I encourage you to work with both as any image that creates a strong energetic charge, whether positive or negative, is a result of our own projection and so has some wisdom to offer us.

Allow yourself a span of time, perhaps twenty or thirty minutes, to let images choose you through this energetic response. Then begin placing them on the mandala in a way that feels satisfying. This is very much an intuitive process; there is no getting it "right."

When you come to the completion of your collage, allow time to simply gaze on it before writing down your experience of the process. Have a dialogue with the images and ask what story they have to share with you.

FOR REFLECTION
- What about Amma Syncletica's story most inspires or energizes you? Where do you feel the strongest connection or disconnection?
- How might you summon forth your inner Warrior? Where in your life do you need stronger boundaries?
- How might you practice "doing battle with thoughts"?
- What did the visual art exploration experience reveal to you?

CLOSING BLESSING
This is a wonderful time to pause and ask how the Warrior helps to illuminate the way ahead. What are the boundaries you are being invited to claim? What are you discovering through this work?

For the poem below I was inspired to write through the voice of Amma Syncletica and imagined myself in her shoes and what her journey and courage must have been like to experience.

Amma's Prayer

I belong to that which cannot be seen.
Scorpion's sting, snake's slow hiss,
heat of the stone cave walls,
a portion of bread meant to last for days,
desert draws forth what is essential in me.

I belong to that which cannot be spoken.
I open my parched mouth to sing,
choke on grit and gravel.
Feeling the grey force of the storm rising,
I am stunned into silence.

I belong to that which cannot be heard.
I lay stretched thin across the landscape's aching silence.
Great fields of darkness invite me to rest a while.
I am borne of bone and breath, flesh and fears,
bitter earth, ground cracked open.

I belong to that which cannot be known.
The sky is burning now, no respite for warriors,
a thousand inner battles under a blazing sun.
Greed, boredom, lust, anger are some of my visitors,
I invite them in for tea scrounged from roots and leaves.

I belong to the One who dwells within.
See, a river of light flows from my lips.
I am she who knows the sun does not rise,
but it is we who stand on the circling earth and
plunge ourselves into that fiery embrace.

May you find the fierceness within to honor and protect that which is most precious. May you find the courage to say no to all that drains and disempowers so your yes may be all the more radiant.

Brigid of Kildare: The Healer

INTRODUCTION TO BRIGID OF KILDARE

St. Brigid (ca. 451–525) is one of Ireland's three patron saints, alongside Patrick and Columba. We don't know many details of her life, and there is great evidence that some of the legends and stories surrounding her are Christian versions of the traditions of the pre-Christian goddess Brigid, who was associated with poets, smithwork, and healing.

Most of what we know about St. Brigid comes from the *Life of St. Brigid* written by the monk Cogitosus in the second half of the seventh century. The *Life* emphasizes her healings, her kinship with animals, her profound sense of hospitality and generosity, and her concern for those oppressed. These stories of the saints are meant to be not literal or historical but spiritual, mythical, archetypal, and psychological, resonating with the deepest parts of our souls.

Her feast day is February 1, which, in the Celtic calendar, is also the feast of Imbolc and the very beginning of springtime. It is the time when the ewes begin to give birth and give forth their milk, and it heralds the coming of longer and warmer days. She is the first sign of life after the long dark nights of winter. She breathes into the landscape so that it begins to awaken. Snow-drops, the first flowers of spring, are one of her symbols.

On the eve of January 31 it is traditional to leave a piece of cloth or ribbon outside the house. It was believed that Brigid's spirit traveled across the land and left her curative powers in the *brat Bride* (Brigid's mantle or cloth). It was then used throughout the year for healing from sickness and protection from harm.

Brigid's feast day is also connected to the Christian liturgical year, followed by the Feast of the Presentation of Jesus on February 2. Spiritual writer and teacher Jan Richardson describes how this day invites us to "remember Mary and Joseph's visit to the Temple to present their child Jesus on the fortieth day following his birth, as Jewish law required, and for Mary to undergo the postpartum rites of cleansing. Luke's Gospel tells us that the prophets Anna and Simeon immediately recognize and welcome Jesus. Taking the child into his arms, Simeon turns his voice toward God and offers praise for the 'light for revelation' that has come into the world."

Jan goes on to write that, inspired by Simeon's words, "some churches began to mark the day with a celebration of light: the Candle Mass, during which priests would bless the candles to be used in the year to come. Coinciding with the turn toward spring and lengthening of light in the Northern Hemisphere, Candlemas offers a liturgical celebration of the renewing of light and life that comes to us in the natural world at this time of year, as well as in the story of Jesus. As we emerge from the deep of winter, the feast reminds us of the perpetual presence of Christ our Light in every season."[1]

In Ireland, Brigid is even called Mary of the Gaels and was said to be present as a midwife to Mary at the birth of Jesus. She cross-es thresholds of time and space, and these stories often break the boundaries of linearity. It is said that she was born as her mother crossed the threshold of a doorway. Women giving birth often stand on the threshold of a doorway and call out her name.

Brigid was a powerful leader and one of the founders of monasticism in Ireland. She was an abbess, healer, soul friend, prophet, and more. Many miracles are connected to her, especially related to milk. She had a white cow who could give as much milk as needed. A small amount of her butter miraculously fed many guests. There is a sense of lavish hospitality and generosity connected to the spirit of Brigid. Many of the stories connected to her reflect the dignity of the ordinary tasks, especially in the home—no more divisions between what is worthy of grace and what is beyond the scope.

There is the story of how Brigid received the land for her monastery in Kildare. She asked for what her mantle would cover and was told she could have that much. When she placed the mantle on the ground, it grew until it covered enough land for the monastery. The word "Kildare" comes from the Irish *cill dara*, which means "church of the oak."

Brigid is especially connected to the elements of water and fire. Many holy wells across Ireland are dedicated to her. Wells are places of healing, where those suffering with illness come to be transformed. In Kildare is the perpetual flame of Brigid. When she was consecrated as a nun (and legend says she was inadvertently also ordained bishop), a flame extended from her head up to the heavens. She is invoked for protection in travel, in prayers at night, and in the work of the day.

Often in Ireland, I have heard Brigid described as a bridge between the pre-Christian and Christian traditions, between the other world and this one. The Healer is the one who bridges gaps and divisions. She can help bring healing to a world divided between religious beliefs. She bridges the natural and human world. Brigid sees the face of Christ in all persons and creatures and

overcomes the division between rich and poor. Our practice of inner hospitality as monks in the world is essentially about healing
all of the places we feel fragmented, scattered, and shamed. One
of her symbols is her cloak, which becomes a symbol of unity. All
can dwell under her mantle.

Brigid believed that having a soul friend, or *anam cara*, was also
an essential part of healing on the spiritual journey. She says anyone without one "is like a body without a head." The soul friend
is the one who helps us to become whole again, who witnesses our
journey with love and compassion, and who challenges us in the
hard places where we fight against ourselves over and over.

I have come to embrace and love Brigid more and more the
longer I live in this sacred landscape of Ireland. From visiting her
holy wells to participating in the festivals for her feast day to sharing in her kinship with creatures, I discover in Brigid a powerful
source of wisdom for how to be with the places within me that
often feel divided. I find myself calling on her name in times of
illness or other places where the gap between my heart's longing
and how I am living feels so very large.

Similar to Mary, she invites us to embrace the feminine face of
the divine. With her connection to the ancient goddess tradition,
Brigid extends the lavish generosity of the Mother to us, but in a
way that calls us to begin to heal all of the broken places so that
we might extend that love and abundance to others. Perhaps we
will discover what was once a wound has been transformed into a
calling out into the world in service to others.

ICON SYMBOLISM: BRIGID OF KILDARE

The quote on the icon, "Christ dwells in every creature," is attributed to Brigid and express the heart of her sense of hospitality
and the sacred dwelling in all things.

In the image, she is accompanied by some of her symbols, including the flame, a Brigid's cross, and a white cow, which was said to accompany her and provide milk for all who needed it.

I invite you to cast a soft gaze on Brigid's image. Allow some time with her presence and see what you receive in your prayer.

THE ARCHETYPE OF THE HEALER

The Healer is the one who helps us to overcome inner divisions of body, mind, soul, heart, and spirit. Healing is very different than curing. Even if an illness does not go away, the Healer within allows us to find some wisdom and grace in the experience and allows us to have some peace and ease in the midst of unknowing and pain.

Similarly, with emotional wounds, the Healer is the one who helps us to welcome the stranger and find reconciliation—perhaps even gratitude for these parts of the self that have for so long vexed us.

Healing is not so much about *doing* but rather about a way of *being* that lies beyond all the false divisions we make in our lives. Healing often inspires radical life changes and brings about ways of being more in alignment with our true Self and nature.

The Healer is not only present in the traditional practice of medicine or other healing arts such as herbalism, massage, energy work, midwifery, and so forth. The Healer also works through spiritual direction, retreat work, psychotherapy, and any way that a person accesses this archetypal aspect of the self to overcome inner divisions.

The heart of healing work is transformation—transforming pain, wounds, self-imposed limitations, grief, and loss, and discovering within them a gift or grace. The process of healing takes time, a lifetime really. Many of our issues will return again and again. This is where conversion reminds us that we are never done.

The wounded Healer, which Henri Nouwen writes so beautifully about, points to the way that our own inner Healer is broken open through our woundedness. We each carry the great wounds of life, but some of us will become victimized by them and let them ultimately tear us apart while some of us will slowly find empowerment and a call to be in service to others. We may resist our wounds, but the ancient stories tell us the wound is where the jewels are hidden. Wounding can become a process of initiation into a way of being that honors the wounds of human life, approaches them with reverence and gentleness, and creates spaces where the wounds are made welcome.

We often seek outside sources for our healing journeys. Ultimately, we must turn within, find the inner Healer at work, and call upon her or his wisdom for us. It can be confusing when we are ill, and there are so many possible modalities for healing. When we pause and turn to the Healer we have inside of us, we can ask for the way forward. This doesn't mean that we don't seek the healing gifts of others but that we don't give away our power to heal in that relationship.

THE SHADOW SIDE OF THE HEALER

The shadow Healer is manifested as someone who takes advantage of others who are wounded, often claiming to have a "miracle" cure. This is rampant in our era of New Age claims about healing. If a person isn't healed, then the blame is often placed on him or her for not thinking the right thoughts or feeling the right feelings. The popular book *The Secret* is one manifestation of this shadow energy in that it ultimately blames people for any misfortune that befalls them and creates a sense of profound guilt in its wake.

It is true that sometimes our body does physically manifest symptoms of the soul, but we must be careful how we approach this truth. The shadow lays blame on the individuals for their suffering and so can distance them from the compassion they need to have for themselves under the circumstances. It also fosters a false sense of control over the unpredictability of life by suggesting what the cause of someone else's suffering might be. In that way we can believe it won't happen to us.

JESUS AND THE HEALER ARCHETYPE: THE RAISING OF LAZARUS
REFLECTION BY JOHN VALTERS PAINTNER

Jesus said, "Take away the stone." Martha, the sister of the dead man, said to him, "Lord, already there is a stench because he has been dead four days." Jesus said to her, "Did I not tell you that if you believed, you would see the glory of God?" So they took away the stone. And Jesus looked upward and said, "Father, I thank you for having heard me. I knew that you always hear me, but I have said this for the sake of the crowd standing here, so that they may believe that you sent me." When he had said this, he cried with a loud voice, "Lazarus, come out!" The dead man came out, his hands and feet bound with strips of cloth, and his face wrapped in a cloth. Jesus said to them, "Unbind him, and let him go."

—John 11:1–44

Begin by reading the whole scripture passage as indicated and then pray with the excerpt in a contemplative way such as lectio divina (see guidelines in the appendix).

Of all of Jesus' miracles, this one is the most personal. Lazarus is not just a stranger in the crowd or the relative of someone he meets. Lazarus is a personal friend; he's practically family. It is the only instance recorded in the gospels where Jesus cries for an individual.

It's an odd story. Jesus ignores the pleading of his disciples and delays his journey to visit the sick Lazarus. He even reassures everyone that the illness won't end in death. But Lazarus does die. He dies four days before Jesus eventually shows up.

When Jesus does finally arrive, Mary confronts him about the delay. And yet she still has faith in Jesus' ability to make things right, to heal what has been broken.

Jesus asks to be taken to where Lazarus has been buried, and he gives a series of commands. Jesus begins by telling the crowd to roll away the stone in front of the tomb. Some warn about the stench of the four-day-old dead body, but Jesus insists. He then cries out in a loud voice for Lazarus to come out of the tomb. Next, Jesus instructs the stunned crowd to untie his friend from the burial wrappings. Finally, he instructs them to let Lazarus go.

There is so much more going on than just Lazarus rising from the dead. The grieving hearts of Lazarus's family and friends are also healed. And then there is the lesson of how Jesus heals. Jesus insists on going to the grave and demands to bear witness to everything, not letting the reality be hidden behind the stone. Like so many other miracles, Jesus requires those afflicted to take some part in their own healing. There is only one set of footprints for part of Lazarus's journey out of the tomb, and they belong to Lazarus. Next, Jesus involves the community in the raising of Lazarus. They must help untie the risen Lazarus who is still bound, for we all need some help at some point. Finally, Jesus instructs the community to allow Lazarus his freedom. No demands of service or payment are placed on Lazarus. He is free to do as he will.

Jesus heals in many ways. He is a healer of physical ailments and of damaged souls. Jesus does this not out of an agenda but out of deep-rooted compassion for the ones afflicted. He makes them whole again simply because that is how God intends them to be.

THE PRACTICE OF THE HOLY PAUSE

We are continually crossing thresholds in our lives, both the literal kind when moving through doorways as well as the metaphorical thresholds when time becomes a transition space of waiting and tending. We hope for news about a friend struggling with illness, or we long for clarity about our own deepest dreams. We await the day when we will no longer feel so torn apart by the great losses of our lives.

In the monastic tradition, *statio* is the practice of stopping one thing before beginning another. It is the acknowledgment that in the space of transition and threshold is a sacred dimension, a holy pause full of possibility. This *place between* is a place of stillness, where we let go of what came before and prepare ourselves to enter fully into what comes next.

When we pause between activities or spaces or moments in our day, we open ourselves to the possibility of discovering a new kind of presence in the "in-between times." When we rush from one thing to another, we skim over the surface of life, losing that sacred attentiveness that brings forth revelations in the most ordinary of moments. Brigid knew the hallowedness of the most mundane tasks. She calls us to stay present to the gifts she brings.

Statio calls us to a sense of reverence for slowness, for mindfulness, and for the fertile dark spaces between our goals where we can pause, center ourselves, and listen. We can open up a space within for God to work. We can become fully conscious of what we are about to do rather than mindlessly completing another task.

We often think of these in-between times as wasted moments and inconveniences rather than opportunities to begin again and again, to awaken to the gifts right here, not the ones we imagine waiting for us beyond the next door.

The holy pause can also be the space of integration and healing. How often do we rush through our lives, not allowing the time to gather the pieces of ourselves, to allow our fragmented selves the space of coming together again? When we allow rest, we awaken to the broken places that often push us to keep doing, producing, and striving.

I imagine the holy hush that descended over Mary and Joseph after she gave birth to her infant son. The sense of wonder and marvel at the miracle that is new life. A friend of mine recently gave birth to her first child in her forties; she wanted this very much. Her son was born twenty-one days late, so there was great anticipation from her as well as family and friends over his arrival. Once her son was born, she asked for two weeks before showing him off to friends because she wanted this sacred time just to be with her baby, to soak in his presence and the gifts he brought her. She was allowing a holy pause to cherish this gift.

MEDITATION: INVITING YOUR INNER HEALER

Find a comfortable position, and begin to breathe slowly. Draw your breath in and out with presence and attention. See if you might find in your breath an ally on this journey of healing as it brings you the gift of life and also helps bring ease and release to your body.

Allow your breath to carry your awareness down to your heart center. Simply notice whatever your experience is right now and welcome it, without judgment or trying to change anything. Welcome this experience as a kind of healing. Simply be with what is.

Welcome in the presence of Brigid into your imagination. See her in whatever way she wants to appear. Perhaps she is wearing her mantle or surrounded by the flames of inspiration or accompanied by her faithful cow. See Brigid point to the presence of the Spirit and the Healer with you in this sacred space. Simply rest with them for a moment. Feel yourself supported and held.

Ask Brigid to show you all the ways you have become divided within yourself. Begin with the places in your body that need healing. Ask for the grace to find ease with your body.

Turn to the places where your thoughts are divided, perhaps the ways you tear yourself or others apart with thoughts of judgment or criticism.

Bring your attention to your heart. Ask to see the places of woundedness, the grief, the sorrow, and the places that call out for reconciliation. It might be someone who hurt you deeply many years ago, it might be an estranged family member, or it might be another experience of wounding. Go gently to these places, just opening to the possibility of healing.

Ask Brigid and your inner Healer to help you to be present to these experiences and to show you the way toward healing these divided places. You do not have to understand how this will come about; just rest in the possibility that there is wisdom beyond your horizon of knowing. Know that this healing wisdom is within you.

Rest in this experience for as long as you need. See if a gesture arises in response to what is unfolding in your prayer.

Once you are ready to return to the outer world, let your breath carry you gently back. Allow a few moments to record your experience and any insights in a journal.

MANDALA EXPLORATION: COLLAGE MANDALAS

We return again to the collage form for our mandala. Gather your images, paper circle, glue stick, and scissors. Find some time for yourself and this visual prayer. Awaken your body through gentle movement and stretching. Spend a few moments before starting to center yourself through your breath. Invite your inner Healer to be present, and ask for whatever grace you seek during this time. Move into the process with intention and reverence.

As you sort through the images, notice again which ones shimmer and which ones repel you. Choose some from both groups. Allow your intuition to guide you as you create the collage and lay out the images. Notice when the inner voices become loud, and see if you can breathe into the moment and let them go.

Once you have come to a place where you feel you have done enough work, rest and enter into some silence with the images. Just be with them for a while before writing about the process.

Enter into dialogue with the images to see what they might teach you about your inner Healer.

FOR REFLECTION

- What about Brigid's story most inspires or energizes you? Where do you feel the strongest connection or disconnection?
- Where do you feel the Healer most at work in your life?
- How might your practice of the holy pause offer you healing grace?
- What are the wounds for which you seek healing? How might those wounds contain the very medicine you are called to offer to the world?
- What did the visual art exploration experience reveal to you?

CLOSING BLESSING

The poem below is based on an image I discovered of Brigid that touched me deeply. The story says she had a heart for those who were suffering, especially the poor, and when she cried, her tears landed on the ground and from that spot a great fruit tree emerged. It is a beautiful symbol of the journey of the Healer from wounded one to one who offers healing and grace to others.

St. Brigid and the Fruit Tree

There was the moment
you could bear it no more.
Your eyes brimming with
great glistening drops
summoned by the hunger of
the world, the callous and
terrible things men and
women do to one another.

Your tears splashed onto
cold stony earth, ringing out
like bells calling monks to prayer,
like the river breaking open to
the wide expanse of sea.

From that salt-soaked ground
a fruit tree sprouts and rises.
I imagine pendulous pears,
tears transmuted to sweetness.

There will always be more grief
than we can bear.
There will always be ripe fruit flesh
making your fingers sticky from the juice.

Life is tidal, rising and receding,
its long loneliness, its lush loveliness,
no need to wish for low tide when
the banks are breaking.

The woman in labor straddles the doorway
screaming out your name.
You stand there on the threshold, weeping,

and pear trees still burst into blossom,
their branches hang so heavy, low,
you don't even have to reach.

May all of your tears be transformed into ripe, sweet fruit. May
you find yourself on the journey toward wholeness with Brigid as
companion and guide. And may the days ahead bring the delight
of these companions to your side again and again.

HELP ME TO JOURNEY BEYOND THE FAMILIAR AND INTO THE UNKNOWN.

BRENDAN THE NAVIGATOR

Brendan the Navigator: The Pilgrim

- -

INTRODUCTION TO BRENDAN THE NAVIGATOR

The Prayer of St. Brendan

Help me to journey beyond the familiar
and into the unknown.
Give me the faith to leave old ways
and break fresh ground with You.
Christ of the mysteries, I trust You
to be stronger than each storm within me.
I will trust in the darkness and know
that my times, even now, are in Your hand.
Tune my spirit to the music of heaven,
and somehow, make my obedience count for You.

I was not that familiar with Brendan the Navigator (ca. 484–ca. 577) until I moved to Ireland. I relish knowing I have walked and sailed on some of the same places as he. Officially, he would be known as Brendan of Clonfert, and there is a cathedral in Clonfert, Ireland, bearing his name and a site said to be his grave.

The "Navigator" or "Voyager" is his more commonly known title because his life was defined by his seven-year-long journey across the sea to find the "Island Promised to the Saints." Before embarking on his journey, he would have visited the island of Inismor off the coast of County Galway to receive a blessing from St. Enda.

He heard the call to search for this mythical island in a dream from an angel who promised to be with him and guide him there. Brendan brought along a group of fellow monks for community and searched for seven years—sailing in circles and visiting many of the islands again and again. Each year he celebrated Easter Mass on the back of a whale. Each year he visited the island of the birds, where white-feathered creatures sang the psalms with his monks. Only when his eyes were opened did he see that the paradise he sought was right with him.

There is, of course, the actual narrative of a physical voyage. Tim Severin, a sailor in the 1970s, re-created the voyage Brendan took, rebuilding the same boat, and landed in places like Iceland and Greenland. There have been suggestions that Brendan was perhaps the first to land in North America. This is the outward geography of the journey.

There is also a deeper, archetypal layer to this journey, which resonates with our own inner Pilgrim—the part of ourselves drawn to make long voyages in search of something for which we long. This is the inward geography of the journey, one where we may physically travel only a few feet or miles but where the soul moves in astronomical measure.

The *Navigatio*, as the text of Brendan's voyage is known in Latin, is a story of a soul rooted deeply in the monastic tradition and culture, as well as the liturgical cycles and rhythms in early medieval Ireland. Each of the various parts of their journey take place in forty- and fifty-day increments to reflect the liturgical

seasons and the rhythms of fasting. They made landfall to celebrate the major feasts and were always accompanied by the singing of the Divine Office and chanting of the psalms. Time is not
linear on this journey. Brendan and his monks moved in circles,
spiraling again and again to familiar places from new perspectives.

This journey is an allegory of spiritual transformation. It tells
of the soul's seeking to live and respond to the world from an
experience of inner transfiguration, with themes of waiting, anticipation, striving, searching, and seeing from a deeper perspective. The heart of the voyage asks us, what needs to change for
the "Land Promised to the Saints" to be recognized? What is
the way required through both illuminated and shadowy interi-
or landscapes? Are we able to stay present through moments of
solace, ease, and joy, as well as the anxiety, fear, and sometimes
terror that comes when we let go of all that is familiar to follow
our heart's calling? Can we see the difficult journey as a passage of
initiation?

There is a great deal of waiting in this journey, and so much unknowing. There are whole seasons when they feel impatient and
confused about why they can't find the place they were seeking
so diligently. Yet it is the very journey through the shadows that
is required to make the desired discovery. Brendan doesn't arrive
to the promised land he seeks until he has completed his arduous
journey within.

In Cynthia Bourgeault's book *Mystical Hope: Trusting in the
Mercy of God*, she reminds us that like the sea voyage Brendan
makes, we too can only reach our destination if we learn to see
in a new way: "As the manuscript makes clear, the land promised
to the saints is reached not only in physical space, but simulta-
neously in *inner space* through the journey of moral and spiritual
purification that prepares the way for the eventual opening of the
eye of the heart."[1]

She goes on to write: "He can find it only when something is reversed inside him. Instead of looking outward for landfalls and destinations, an inner eye opens within Brendan that can see the luminous fullness of the Land Promised to the Saints always and everywhere present beneath the surface motions of coming, going, striving, arriving."[2]

This world Brendan seeks and discovers is more of a quality than a physical landmark: "world within a world—not the physical place itself, but the quality of aliveness in it . . . the land itself was merely the outer shell; it was the live holiness dancing within it that created the beauty."[3]

"You are the veil that hides the paradise you seek" is a quote attributed to St. Brendan. The longest journey seems to be the letting go of the expectations, the assumptions, and the woundings, all of the ways we seek just what we are looking for rather than what is waiting to be revealed. In many ways, this is a continuation of our practice of yielding, which we explored in the last chapter, and releasing our expectations, following the current of where life is carrying us.

Cynthia Bourgeault would claim that it was Brendan's spiritual practice as a monk—the chanting of the psalms, lectio divina, and commitment to nurturing times of silence and being in community—which transformed his heart along the way. These are the practices that open us within to something beyond what we can see or name.

ICON SYMBOLISM: BRENDAN THE NAVIGATOR

"Help me to journey beyond the familiar and into the unknown" is from a prayer attributed to St. Brendan that I shared in the opening of this reflection. This is the heart of the journey Brendan makes, a release of what he wants to have happen into what is actually unfolding.

In this icon he is depicted celebrating Easter Mass on the back of a whale, which paints a most delightful scene to imagine. He returns there each year while on his seven-year voyage. The icon also depicts the boat that would have carried him and his monks across the sea for seven long years.

THE ARCHETYPE OF THE PILGRIM

The Pilgrim embarks on an outward journey with inward significance, seeking wisdom and an encounter with the divine in what Celtic spirituality names as thin places, where the landscape brings one closer to the divine presence because the veils are thin.

When I teach about the expressive arts, I often use pilgrimage as a metaphor for what happens in the process of art-making. When we enter the creative process we first prepare for the time, bless our journey, and then step in without knowing where it will take us. Each moment in the unfolding becomes an opportunity for the discovery of who we are and who God is in our lives.

Staying with the process and attending to it means letting go of our expectations of how things will turn out. It means letting go of destinations. Sometimes the Pilgrim sets out with a particular destination in mind, as did Brendan, but it is always the journey along the way that unsettles the assumptions and opens us to new possibilities beyond our own imagining.

The Pilgrim is one who actually courts holy disruption, seeks to get lost, and opens oneself up to the strangeness of being in a foreign land, knowing that all of this discomfort will break one open in new ways. One of my favorite quotes is from Phil Cousineau's book *The Art of Pilgrimage: The Seeker's Guide to Making Travel Sacred*: "If your journey is indeed a pilgrimage, a soulful journey, it will be rigorous. Ancient wisdom suggests if you aren't trembling as you approach the sacred, it isn't the real thing. The sacred, in its various guises as holy ground, art, or knowledge, evokes emotion *and* commotion."[4]

The Pilgrim is not going on a vacation to relax and unwind from the stresses of daily living. People have been called to make these kinds of sacred journeys for centuries, perhaps much longer. It is an archetypal impulse, a deep knowing that traveling, seeking, and immersing oneself in strangeness can bring about profound inner transformation.

Each moment brings a new invitation. Can we stay present enough to see what is actually showing up in this moment rather than being attached to how we want things to be?

In the midst of the discomfort that a pilgrimage brings into our lives, we can be heartened to know that the journey is also a prayer, and prayer does not promise ease or comfort. The inner Pilgrim knows this is a sacred experience. We perhaps find solace in knowing that all of the stories of inner discovery come through a radical undoing of our own agendas and a call to stay with the unknowing for much longer than we would want to.

Ultimately, we are making the journey from an ego-driven life to one that is soul-drawn. As the voyage strips away our sense of control and what is important, our values become reoriented after a profound disorientation. The archetype of the Pilgrim demands nothing less from us.

THE SHADOW SIDE OF THE PILGRIM

The shadow Pilgrim is manifested when the focus becomes the striving itself or when we lose sight of what we are seeking and wander aimlessly. While we certainly need to hold the destination loosely, the aim is always to follow the unfolding call of the Spirit.

The shadow side of the Pilgrim is often expressed when we use a journey to run from our problems. We live in a highly mobile culture, and we have an often overwhelming array of choices for where to live, what practices to take on for our spiritual lives, and so on. A great voyage, whether it be actual travel or a diverting pursuit of some kind, can be a way of avoiding a deeply rooted wound that needs care and attention. We don't need to travel very far to disconnect from what is most challenging in our own lives.

The shadow Pilgrim can also emerge when we embark on a pilgrimage because there is a certain mystique about it. Spiritual pilgrimage has become a very popular endeavor, but we can make an entire outward journey without ever really changing our inward direction. Pilgrimage can become an activity of consumption or spiritual conquest. Perhaps we like the way it sounds to say we have been on such a journey and the sense of importance or status it conveys.

The shadow Pilgrim can emerge if we exclusively focus on what we think should happen and miss out on the gifts along the way that are the actual purpose of the journey. Or we may try to control every step, plan every moment, so there is never any possibility of discomfort or getting lost that might shake us up.

We also find the shadow in the belief that we need to make the journey alone or that no one understands the struggles we are experiencing. The Pilgrim is always a pilgrim-in-community.

JESUS AND THE PILGRIM ARCHETYPE: THE ROAD TO EMMAUS
REFLECTION BY JOHN VALTERS PAINTNER

Now on that same day two of them were going to a village called Emmaus, about seven miles from Jerusalem, and talking with each other about all these things that had happened. While they were talking and discussing,

Jesus himself came near and went with them.

—Luke 24:13–35

Begin by reading the whole scripture passage as indicated and then pray with the excerpt in a contemplative way such as lectio divina (see guidelines in the appendix).

Shortly after Jesus' arrest and execution, his followers were either in hiding or on the run. In this story, two of his disciples are leaving Jerusalem. They encounter a fellow traveler along the way. Eventually the conversation turns to current events, and the two are shocked that this stranger hasn't heard what has been happening in Jerusalem the past few days. They begin to explain about Jesus but are surprised when the stranger begins to tell them about Jesus and the prophecies in scripture. They are so consumed by the conversation that they plead for their new traveling companion to stop with them for the night and share a meal. Only in the breaking of the bread do they recognize the risen Christ.

The gospel doesn't tell us exactly where Cleopas and his companion are heading or why. That they have a destination in mind is clear. That their journey is derailed by a great spiritual enlightenment is even clearer.

We don't know much about them. Many have speculated that Cleopas's unnamed companion may have been a woman, a relative or spouse. Classical paintings depict the two disciples as men, but that is an artistic interpretation and not a literal visual translation of what's in the scripture. We do know that the two are not members of the innermost circle of the twelve apostles, and yet they do have intimate knowledge of what happened to Jesus and who he was. Do they not recognize Jesus because they had not previously met him, only knowing him by reputation?

We also know that they are bold to speak so openly about Jesus' arrest and execution to one they consider a stranger. They are good listeners, taking in much as they share in the conversation.

Cleopas and his companion are also very hospitable. They ask this stranger to stay and dine with them. It is another risk on their part, but their hearts were on fire for greater wisdom from their new traveling companion. And it is in the sharing of a meal, an ancient custom of connectedness and honoring of one another, that their eyes are fully opened. Finally, they complete their journey by immediately returning to the community and sharing the gift they have received.

This story is so typical of Jesus' many journeys. He rarely travels alone and always connects with those he meets along the way. He walks and talks and shares with everyone, leaving them richer for having met him. Where Jesus goes is not nearly as important as those he meets along the way. He has the heart of a Pilgrim.

THE PRACTICE OF CONVERSION

We are always beginners on the spiritual journey. The practice of conversion calls us to remember this. The Pilgrim calls us to remember the ongoing unfolding of life.

When we embrace our inner Pilgrim we begin to see all of life as a process of revelation, of holy moments, and of new possibilities arising that we could not have expected. I like to think of conversion as a commitment to always being surprised by God. When we lose this capacity for awe and wonder we become cynical and think we have seen it all. Our hearts grow hard to the new possibilities. This is a lifelong commitment. In this lifetime we never arrive at our ultimate destination, so that is not the goal, but we can discover that home or the promised land is just beneath the surface of life right here and now (especially when the Visionary steps in to help us illuminate this reality).

This is what Brendan as Pilgrim ultimately had to learn. He was seeking this place, but he found himself going in circles. He had to allow himself to become disoriented, to be with the discomfort of waiting, to attend to what was actually happening rather than what he desired. Embracing these facets of the spiritual life is essential to conversion.

The Pilgrim invites us to lean into mystery and wait. It calls us not only to let go of our own agendas for this time but also to show up to the holy practice of tending, listening, and remembering that there is always something new awaiting us.

MEDITATION: INVITING YOUR INNER PILGRIM

Allow a few moments to settle into your body, noticing any places of tightness or holding. Deepen your breath, letting your inhale and exhale be long and slow. Sit in this place of arriving for a few moments, drawing your attention and energy inward, following the inhale of your breath into your center and with the exhale simply releasing any anxiety or distraction as much as possible.

Invite in the presence of Brendan the Navigator. See him surrounded by his community of monks standing there on the boat being carried by the waves. See him inviting you to embark on your own great voyage of the heart. Brendan points to the Spirit who is the true guide for this journey, not our own agendas or needs. Let both the Spirit and your needs be with you as you listen more deeply.

See yourself stepping onto the boat. Experience the disorientation that comes with its rocking back and forth. Breathe in and out any anxiety that arises, and allow yourself to soften into its rhythm.

Feel your body relax, scanning gently to find any places of tightness or clenching. Imagine yourself floating gently along with the current. Allow yourself to feel carried in a holy direction, even if you have no idea what that might be. Sit for several moments with this experience of unknowing; welcome your heart's deep longing for a more intimate encounter with the divine presence and your own soul's calling.

Bring this insight to Brendan and the Spirit's wisdom. Open up to their response, which may not come in words. Ask for their blessing of this journey. See if a gesture arises in your body as a physical symbol of this prayer and then carry that offering with you this day.

When you are ready to end this meditation time, deepen into your breath and allow your inhale and exhale to gently move you from this inner space back to an outer awareness. Allow some time for journaling, writing anything that arose or surprised you.

MANDALA EXPLORATION:
PHOTOGRAPHY MANDALAS

You are invited for this exploration to go on a contemplative walk. This is a walk without a particular destination in mind; simply be present to how your journey unfolds step by step. Bring a camera with you; if you have one on your phone that is fine.

Begin by allowing a few moments to center yourself through breathing. Draw your awareness from your head down to your heart. The heart is a place of receptivity and welcome to whatever comes. You will be walking from a heart-centered place, where instead of "taking" photos, we will be open to "receiving" them as gifts that come to us. As you walk soften your gaze. This means not to grasp at things you see but to honor them with reverence and gratitude.

Call upon your inner Pilgrim to guide you on this journey and listen for where you are being directed. Let the Spirit lead the journey rather than trying to get somewhere in particular.

When something catches your attention, try framing it with the camera as a way of honoring the moment. Pay special attention to the places where mandalas or circular shapes appear in the world around you in the form of signs, architecture, and nature, anywhere they might appear.

Walk for as long as you feel led. When you return home, allow a few minutes to simply sit in silence. Then spend some time gazing on the images you received.

FOR REFLECTION

- What about Brendan's story most inspires or energizes you? Where do you feel the strongest connection or disconnection?
- How does your inner Pilgrim express her- or himself in your life?
- Where does your inner Pilgrim long to journey?
- How might you practice conversion and allow yourself to be surprised by life?
- What did the visual art exploration experience reveal to you?

CLOSING BLESSING

One of my favorite stories from the *Navigatio* is when Brendan and his monks leave the whale upon which they celebrated Easter Mass (first thinking it was just an island) and then landed on an island where the trees were covered with white-feathered birds, so many that they could not even see the branches. These birds then joined in chorus to sing the Divine Office with the monks—such an incredible image of Earth as original monastery and nature joining in the praise of the divine presence everywhere!

St. Brendan and the Songbirds

Imagine the hubris, searching for the saint-promised island,
the stubbornness to continue for seven journeys around the sun.
Each day on the rolling sea, his fellow monks
jostled and tossed by waves.

Brendan asks late one evening:
How will I know when I find what I seek?
Easter Sunday brings liturgy on the back of a whale,
but as if that weren't miracle enough, they travel onward.

The ship is tossed onto sand and stone.
They look up to behold a broad and magnificent
oak frosted with white birds hiding the branches entirely,
downy tree limbs reaching upward.

The monks stand huddled under a blue stone sky
relieved to be on stable earth for now.
The sun descends, Vespers, rose to lavender to violet,
heralding the great night's arrival.

They release a collective sigh of contentment, the air expands
around them as a thousand snowy birds ascend into that
newly hollowed space, and throats open together,
a human-avian chorus of shared devotion to the ancient songs.

Ever eager to journey forward, Brendan still lingers for fifty days
sitting in that oak cathedral, feathers scribing their own sacred texts.
In those moments, did the relentless seeking fall away,
sliding off like the veil hiding a bride's expectant face?

Blessings as you continue to journey toward your own holy birthing. May you find the courage to throw away your oars and allow the wind and current to carry you to the promised land. May your own seeking heart find rest in the moments of revelation that arise along the way.

LET OUR HEARTS OVERFLOW WITH THE INEXPRESSIBLE DELIGHT OF LOVE

THE RULE OF SAINT BENEDICT

BENEDICT OF NURSIA

Benedict of Nursia: The Sage

. . . .

INTRODUCTION TO BENEDICT OF NURSIA

But as we progress in this way of life and in faith,
we shall run on the path of God's commandments,
our hearts overflowing with the inexpressible delight of love.
—*The* Rule *of Benedict*

I have great fondness for St. Benedict (ca. 480–543). As a Benedictine Oblate, I have made a commitment as a lay person to live out a way of life reflected in the *Rule* of Benedict, which has been one of the most enduring and widespread monastic rules of life because of its wisdom and balance.

I first fell in love with him and the path of Benedictine spirituality through Hildegard of Bingen. Her many gifts as an artist and visionary captivated me, and I wanted to know more about the spiritual path that was so foundational to her vision. In graduate school I was gifted with the opportunity to teach an introductory course on Benedictine spirituality and loved the opportunity to dive more deeply into this wisdom in a community of learners.

Later I read two books by Mary Earle for those living with chronic illness that helped me fall even more in love with the

Rule's commitment to balance, moderation, and finding a healing rhythm to life: *Beginning Again: Benedictine Wisdom for Living with Illness and Broken Body* and *Healing Spirit: Lectio Divina and Living with Illness*. I had struggled with rheumatoid arthritis for much of my twenties. I still have the disease, but it is mostly controlled with medication. The Benedictine path helped me to claim the contemplative way, which I saw was not only more true to my nature but also more nourishing of a life lived with physical limitations. When I first moved to Seattle in 2003, I found a Benedictine monastery an hour away, St. Placid Priory, where I became an oblate. I am still affiliated there even though I now live thousands of miles away.

The only information we have about Benedict's life comes from the second book of *Dialogues of Gregory the Great*, which gives you a rough overview of significant moments and miracles attributed to Benedict. Keep in mind, as with all hagiographies, the purpose was to present not a historically accurate and factual portrayal but one to inspire faith and assure of the holiness of this man.

Like many monks, Benedict began as a hermit, living in a cave in Subiaco, Italy, for three years until others began to seek him out for wisdom and asked him to found a community. In 2009 I had the great privilege to make a pilgrimage to Rome for the World Congress of Benedictine Oblates, an amazing gathering of fellow oblates from around the world. As a part of the Congress we visited Subiaco, which is now a monastery built into the side of a hill. You can enter the cave where Benedict is said to have lived. There is a special spirit to the place.

As a part of this experience we also visited Monte Cassino, which is the central monastery he founded high upon a hill. It is now a large and flourishing place where many pilgrims and tourists seeking spiritual connection come. I still treasure my Benedict medal from there that I wear daily around my neck.

Apart from the *Dialogues* where we learn a bit about legends of Benedict's life, we also have the *Rule* of Benedict as the other primary source of information about him. "Listen with the ear of your heart" is the first line of the *Rule*, an invitation to read the words that follow not just with the mind as one learns intellectually but with the heart as one learns things of the soul.

There is much emphasis in the *Rule* on silence and listening closely, on only speaking when we have something to say, rather than trying to fill the quiet. Benedict knew we can hear things in the silence that otherwise gets drowned out with the daily hum. This was an issue even back in the sixth century, long before our endless connectivity online.

The *Rule* has endured because of its balance and wisdom. Clearly it was written out of many years of lived experience with others. Benedict cautions against grumbling in a community, the kind of chatter that can create all kinds of friction and dissatisfaction among members and is ultimately poisonous to its flourishing. He calls us to be mindful of our attitudes to life and how we express them.

Benedict's *Rule* outlines a very practice-oriented life centered on daily lectio divina with the scriptures and other wisdom texts, time for silence, solitude, and quiet meditation, as well as following the rhythm of the Liturgy of the Hours and entering into the rise and fall of each day. When the monastery bells rang, monks were expected to drop what they were doing and come straight to prayer as a way of ordering their priorities. The Hours were usually sung prayers, a chanting of the Psalms, the ancient voice of the Jewish tradition, and so offering an unbroken chain of prayer.

The three vows Benedictines would take were obedience, conversion, and stability. The root of the word obedience means to listen, encouraging a deep listening and responsiveness to life. On one level it is obedience to an abbot or abbess and God, but true obedience is always about turning deeply within to hear the invitation being offered uniquely to you in this moment and then having the courage to say yes. Conversion is about an openness to being surprised by God. Stability is the call to stay in the moment. It calls us not to run away when things become difficult, whether running physically by packing up and moving or running emotionally by becoming distant or inaccessible to others. Near the end of the *Rule*, Benedict writes, "Whoever you are then (follow) this little rule written for beginners" (*Rule* 73:8). Humility is key for him, the practice of being rooted in our earthiness and acknowledging our limitations. Humility reminds us that we are always on a journey, we are always beginners, especially when it comes to the spiritual path. We lose sight of the wisdom offered to us when we think we have seen or done it all or when we think we have finally arrived.

Benedict invites us into a very earthy life that celebrates the grace in each moment. He writes that the kitchen utensils are to be treated as sacred just like the tools of the altar, so all things are to be approached with reverence. Each guest is to be treated honorably as the face of Christ, so each person is a window to the divine. Each hour of the day brings the opportunity for grace and encounter with God, so all time is holy. This is the hallmark of the Benedictine way, a life that sees everything—each person, every moment, and every encounter—as shimmering with the presence of grace.

Ultimately, Benedict calls us to a life of deepened wisdom that comes through this kind of reverent attention to all life brings. The ability to welcome all of life and stay present to it is what carves out wisdom in the deepest parts of our being and helps us to come to know the depth of mystery at the heart of things.

ICON SYMBOLISM: BENEDICT OF NURSIA

The quote "let our hearts overflow with the inexpressible delight of love" comes from the *Rule* of Benedict. The *Rule* is largely practical in nature, giving solid wisdom and guidance for monks living in community. But there are some lines like this one that express the overarching spirituality of the *Rule* and Benedict's first intention for living the spiritual life. Our practice is always rooted in a love that overflows with delight.

In the image he is holding a copy of the *Rule* of Benedict, an enduring and far-reaching text still offering guidance to monasteries and oblates. He is accompanied by a crow as this bird was his companion and helped to save him from an incident where other monks tried to poison him. In ancient monastic tradition, this kind of kinship with creatures was a sign of holiness. The sun rises behind him because the Liturgy of the Hours were so significant to the rhythm of his day with dawn being one of the special thresholds to awakening.

THE ARCHETYPE OF THE SAGE

The Sage is the One within us who holds immense wisdom. We often look outside ourselves for wisdom, seeking others who can offer us guidance on the path. Certainly turning to ancient texts and practices, as well as elders who have traveled the way, can offer us great riches. But it is to our detriment when we let this substitute for the voice of the wise one within.

Ultimately, we gain wisdom from life experience. It isn't learned through intellect or reading books (as much as we might hope this to be true with our shelves heavy with tomes). Wisdom comes through navigating life experiences that stretch us, push us to our edges, all the while staying as present as possible and not running away. We must keep our heart open to life's tensions, unbearable unknowing, and the incredible paradoxes offered in each moment. Wisdom allows us to hold all of it without needing to come to conclusions or make final black-and-white statements about our experience.

Wisdom is sometimes described as "horizontal revelation" by scripture scholars because it emerges from observations of daily life. The Hebrew scriptures are filled with Wisdom books: Psalms, Song of Songs, Job, Proverbs, Ecclesiastes, and the book of Wisdom. These texts show us how to stimulate our own reflection rather than provide us with answers. Wisdom means we are given responsibility for making choices and often have to act without certainty of the outcome. This is an inherent aspect of life's messiness.

The Sage is the part of ourselves that is seeking truth. The Sage doesn't need to change the world but simply strives to be present to what is. Contemplation has been described by Carmelite William McNamara as a "long loving look at the real." The "real" is the truth of this moment. Contemplation doesn't always lead to savoring beautiful things; sometimes reality is harsh and painful. The question is, can we stay present to our experience of it or do we work subtly to numb ourselves to the truth? Do we think if we can only find the right practice, the right program, or the right teacher, we will find the truth? Or do we remember that the truth is found within?

In yoga philosophy, *satya* means truth. When we come to the mat or the meditation cushion, we are practicing being with the "is-ness" of reality. We cultivate clarity so that we can see more deeply into the truth of our experience. The poet Jane Hirshfield describes this as "the still heart that refuses nothing" in her poem "Lake and Maple." Our inner Sage helps us to reach a place of equanimity wrought from engagement with life. And from this still heart, we can learn to "refuse nothing," which also means to embrace the truth of what is.

I had practiced an open-hearted welcome to my own difficult feelings and experiences for years before I realized that there was still buried within me a desire to have this act of welcoming grief or anger move me forward to a sense of joy or something other than what I was feeling. There is a very subtle way that our presence to our pain for the sake of what we hope comes after still causes us to avoid the truth of this moment. It was really the line from Jane Hirshfield's poem that broke it open for me in a deeper way. The still heart, which is what we are trying to cultivate through contemplation, refuses nothing. The still heart embraces the truth of this moment.

As we develop our ability to move into the silence of the heart we grow in our capacity to live from our inner Sage. We are able, more and more, to welcome in all aspects of our experience, even—or especially—in the midst of life's messiness, challenge, and unknowing. Refusing nothing means making room for the equal measure of sorrow and ecstasy that shower us daily. In the riches of silence, it is all there with us, and we experience a sense of contentment and equanimity.

Ultimately, the Sage helps us cultivate inner freedom from our illusions. We learn how to see and bear the truth. We come to recognize that we are always on a journey of learning. We don't once and for all arrive enlightened, but we are beginners the whole way, as Benedict wisely counsels. My own life-wisdom has emerged from the grief of living: from the times of profound loss, from the experiences of deep fear, and from the moments when I was called upon to bring my whole self to the present and confront the reality that much of life is beyond my control.

A spiritual path rooted in wisdom is practice-centered. Practices that nurture your heart and your connection with your own true voice cultivate your receptivity to meaning and to deeper questions rather than simple answers.

THE SHADOW SIDE OF THE SAGE

This is often where the "golden shadow" emerges that Jung described as those "positive" elements of ourselves that we deny but project onto other people. We are often quick to honor the wisdom of others, to seek wisdom outside of ourselves, but this can be the shadow at work when we forget we contain the wisdom we need.

The dark shadow of the Sage is manifested in different ways. One aspect is an addiction to being right or perfect. The shadow Sage has little tolerance for human frailties and always insists that we are not good enough.

Another aspect of the shadow side is becoming obsessed with figuring out all of life's choices through rational thought. This is an attempt at control, to figure out how things should work based on a linear and logical set of rules about how the world operates. Valuing scientific and empirical knowledge over all else and making no room for intuitive or mystical experience is the shadow Sage at work.

The shadow Sage can also become so obsessed with "non-attachment" that an unhealthy numbness to life is cultivated. Meditation is about cutting through illusion and seeking a deeper truth while experiencing a sense of centeredness in the midst of chaos; however, part of the practice is to let the experience of sorrow or anger or whatever strong emotion is arising move through you, to fully experience it without letting it carry you away. The shadow Sage keeps us detached so we never enter into life's messiness.

· ·

JESUS AND THE SAGE ARCHETYPE: THE PARABLE OF THE TREASURE
REFLECTION BY JOHN VALTERS PAINTNER

The kingdom of heaven is like a treasure hidden in a field, which someone found and hid; then in his joy he goes and sells all that he has and buys that field.

—Matthew 13:44–52

Begin by reading the whole scripture passage as indicated and then pray with the excerpt in a contemplative way such as lectio divina (see guidelines in the appendix).

Earlier in this chapter of Matthew's gospel, Jesus explains the purpose of his parables. Even more than teaching the groups who come to see and hear him, Jesus wants the apostles to understand what he is saying and why. Jesus knows that one day they will be on their own to continue his work.

A recurring theme of Jesus' parables is a reversal of the "conventional wisdom" of the day. There are often surprise endings. Jesus begins with a story using familiar settings for his audience. But just when they assume they know where the story is heading, Jesus challenges their perception by turning the crowd's expectations.

In the first two parables from this section, Jesus talks of individuals who sell everything in order to purchase a great treasure. While the potential pay-off for these two is great, greater than their initial investment, what they invest is everything they have. The risk is enormous. The consequence of failure is catastrophic. And yet risking everything, holding nothing back for a rainy day emergency, is the wise course of action. So assured are they of the treasure's value, that to not risk everything would be the foolish option.

The next parable is about the fishermen's great catch. Everything is caught up in the net. When the haul is brought ashore, the good is separated from the bad. Then the good is stored away and the bad tossed aside. Jesus likens the fishermen to angels, separating the just from the wicked. The righteous are gathered together, while the wicked are tossed into the flames. (Heaven and hell are not named, specifically, but this is one of the passages that give rise to the image of the "fiery pits of hell" popularized by later authors and theologians.)

Finally, Jesus ends by asking if the disciples understood him. And even though they say that they do, Jesus emphasizes the lesson with another parable.

The wisdom Jesus portrays is that of one who, while aware of the world around him, is focused more on how things should be rather than on how they are. There is not a rush to judgment, but when things are clear, decisive action is taken. Jesus' wisdom is not a head, theoretical wisdom. He is a Sage of the people, a practical Sage who challenges the conventional wisdom with the true wisdom of God.

THE PRACTICE OF OBEDIENCE

The root of the word obedience means "to hear," and this vow that Benedictines make is about committing to listen for God's voice in the world and to respond when you hear the call. Obedience is a difficult concept for modern Western thinkers, but consider it as a way of deep listening for the holy in all dimensions of your life. While monks were committed to obedience to their abbot or abbess, at a deeper level, it was about listening for how the divine was calling in the midst of everyday life.

The second part of this listening is a response—are we willing to not only make the time and space to listen for God's call but also respond with our full selves? Esther de Waal describes it as hearing and then acting upon what we have heard, or to "see that listening achieves its aim." The paradoxical outcome of obedience is an inner freedom because we slowly learn to distinguish God's voice from the many other voices that demand our attention.

Obedience calls us to tune into the inner Sage and listen to our wisdom as it rises up in the midst of life circumstances.

MEDITATION: INVITING YOUR INNER SAGE

Find a comfortable seat and begin to move inward. Draw your breath in and out slowly, letting it draw you to a place of stillness and centeredness. Become present to this moment now, just allowing yourself to be with the truth of whatever you are experiencing. Notice what feelings arise. Can you be with them without trying to change them? Can you honor the truth of your experience whatever that might be?

Invite the presence of Benedict of Nursia. See him surrounded by thousands upon thousands of monks who have followed in his footsteps over the last 1,500 years and the current movement of oblates making a commitment to live out this path in daily life beyond the walls of the monastery. Benedict points toward the Spirit who is the ultimate source of wisdom. They are here to support you in listening and being present.

The Pilgrim may have called you out onto unstable ground, a rocking boat, and asked you to trust, to simply allow yourself to follow the current as it carried you. See if you can recall this experience back into your body, staying grounded with your breath.

Then notice what feelings arise in response. Does fear come up that you want to push away? Does resistance arise that you try to deny is there? Does a desire for control arise so that you feel seized by it? Just be present to whatever happens right now, honoring the truth of your experience. Invite your inner Sage to accompany you. Your Sage knows that right in this moment you have everything you need for your journey. Breathe into whatever is flowing through you right now, and see if you can open yourself to this ancient and timeless wisdom that exists within you and that is there to help you stay present, to stay open-hearted, to simply stay.

Invite Benedict and the Spirit to join you as well, knowing you can call on these three at any time to support you in being with the truth of your experience, especially when you would rather the truth were something else. Ask for their blessing of this longing you carry. See if a gesture arises in your body as a physical symbol of this prayer and then hold that offering with you this day.

When you are ready to move back out into the world, let your breath gently carry you and allow a few moments of transition time, journaling any insights or images that arose.

MANDALA EXPLORATION: PHOTOGRAPHY MANDALAS

You are again invited to a contemplative walk experience. Gather your camera, and prepare yourself by centering with your breath and bringing your awareness to your heart. Invite your inner Sage to be with you in this journey, guiding the way. Ask for whatever grace you desire during this time of exploration.

As you walk, pay attention to moments that shimmer forth, meaning things that call forth to you. Bring a sense of holy curiosity to whatever it is that wants you to spend some time with it, looking lovingly from all angles.

You might look again for mandalas that appear in the world around you, or another option is to receive whatever images come and then when you return home, create a mandala from them either digitally on a computer or by printing them out and arranging them as a collage.

FOR REFLECTION

- What about Benedict's story most inspires or energizes you? Where do you feel the strongest connection or disconnection?

- Where are the places in your life where you look for the right answer or the most logical choice and ignore the deeper voice calling to you? When do you question your own "gut instincts"?

- How might you practice obedience and listening to the deep wisdom already within you?

- What did the visual art exploration experience reveal to you?

CLOSING BLESSING

The poem that follows is based on a story from the *Dialogues* of Benedict and his twin sister Scholastica. It is the only place in the text where she appears, but she has a significant impact. The story says that the two of them would gather annually to see one another and share some time together. Scholastica was also the founder of monastic communities. The hour gets late and Benedict needs to return home, as his own *Rule* says that monks should not be out overnight. But Scholastica will have none of this and begins to weep openly, and her grief calls forth a great rainstorm that forces Benedict to stay. The story tells us she dies very soon after, so perhaps she knew what was most important to cherish in that moment. I love it as a story of how even great Rules are meant to sometimes be broken in favor of love.

St. Benedict and the Rainstorm

Early February evening.
Benedict and his twin sister, Scholastica,
talk for hours about dealing with wayward
monks, childhood memories, regrets, and how they
sometimes steal away to the forest to dance.

The beeswax candle extinguished, she
went to fetch another, dinner plates
pushed aside with drips of grease left from
roast chicken, celebrating this yearly
time together, the extra jug of wine nearly emptied.

He gets up to leave but she protests.
Benedict's own *Rule* requires him
to be back at his monastery overnight.
Perhaps she knew she would die only three days later.
Or maybe the rose-hued glimmer of evening astonished her.

Or this was one of those moments she just wished
would linger on, her brother's beard shining
silver in the growing moonlight, wanting to
remember the great brown kindness of his eyes,
feeling the rough warmth of his hands in hers.

Her tears rise up, falling in great splashes,
her weeping calls forth a fierce rainstorm.
Cosmic forces come down on the side of love,
demanding that self-set rules be broken.

I imagine the two of them listening to
the relentless rain beating down around them,
Benedict yielding to the moment, suddenly
seeing the necessity of riverbanks, but also the
widening expanse into the sea.

Perhaps that night they each dreamt that the river
swelled so high it lifted them to the blue bowl of sky,
until the horizon hallowed them.

Until he could see far beyond the stone walls
he had so carefully built.

May you continue to experience the wisdom of love in your
own life. May your Sage carry you to all the places that bring your
heart alive. May you see past the walls of your own life out to the
fields and oceans calling to you.

ALL THE WOMEN WENT OUT AFTER HER WITH TAMBOURINES AND DANCING

PROPHET MIRIAM

Miriam: The Prophet

. . . .

INTRODUCTION TO MIRIAM

The Song of Miriam

*Then the prophet Miriam, Aaron's sister, took a tambourine in her hand; and all
the women went out after her with tambourines and with dancing. And Miriam
sang to them:*
"Sing to the LORD, for he has triumphed gloriously;
horse and rider he has thrown into the sea."

–Exodus 15:20–21

There are six women, including Miriam, in the scriptures given
the name of prophet, five in the Hebrew scriptures and one in the
Christian scriptures. We don't have very many texts about Miriam or her direct teachings. She first appears in the Torah anonymously as the older sister of Moses who stands on the riverbank,
watching to see what would happen to her brother Moses after
their mother placed him in a basket and floated him away.

Later in her life, after generations of enslavement by the Pharaoh, God acts on behalf of the people and sends the plagues
(which mirror the gods of Egypt) to help free them. They get
progressively worse and more threatening (the Death of the First
Born only occurs after the Pharaoh threatens to kill Moses and

Aaron), until the Israelites are able to flee. In the desert of Egypt, God leads them by day as a column of cloud and protects them from the advancing Egyptian army at night as a pillar of fire. At the Sea of Reeds, the waters are parted for them so they are able to escape to freedom but come crashing back on the horses and Egyptian soldiers giving chase.

You might imagine this scene and feel it viscerally. Imagine yourself running for your life with your community, knowing that if you slow down you will be sent back to slavery or perhaps even death. And while the celebration of God killing the Egyptian soldiers may feel repellant, we can look at the story from an archetypal perspective and see the divine presence at work here in favor of freedom rather than slavery, doing what is necessary to allow freedom to thrive.

Arriving on the shores of the other side, it is written that Miriam takes out her tambourine and leads the women in a public celebration and worship of this God of liberation. In the midrashic texts, the ancient rabbis give great praise to Miriam for her tremendous trust in God, reflected by the very fact that she was carrying her tambourine with her in anticipation of the celebration. We can imagine her forethought: in the act of packing whatever she could bring in that hurried exit from Egypt, her tambourine felt like an essential. It is reflective of the depth of her trust that they would be liberated and there would be cause for music and dancing.

In that moment of unbridled joy, they are on a threshold as a people. As we know, the story says they continue wandering for forty years in the wilderness trying to reach the Promised Land. They will grumble many times over their hunger and discomfort and even reflect longingly on their time back in Egypt when they at least had food and shelter guaranteed. But none of that matters in this pause to celebrate the gifts so generously given. They will return to their human ways soon, but in that moment they touch the divine grace in a fully embodied way.

I love that in the limited texts we actually have about Miriam, this is one of the most significant. It is believed that this Canticle of Miriam may be the oldest written portion of the Hebrew scripture. And here she is clearly a leader in the community and enacts a ritual to mark the importance of the occasion. Her tools are music and dance to unleash the joy that this moment deserves in response. With her given title in the scriptures as "prophet," we can savor this role of the Prophet—to name the divine liberation and invite the community into a ritual that helps them to experience this more fully.

The ancient rabbis told of three great gifts that sustained the Jewish people in their long pilgrimage through the desert: the manna, the cloud of glory, and the well, attributed to the three siblings and leaders Moses, Aaron, and Miriam respectively, showing her in full partnership with her brothers.

The tradition of "Miriam's Well" arises from the text that announces her death, followed by a note that the Israelites had run out of water to drink (Nm 20:1–2). The association of these two events led to the writing of midrashic texts by the rabbis, who developed the legend of the abundant well of fresh water that followed Miriam. It is said that it was created on the eve of the first Sabbath, a gift of replenishment.

According to the tradition, the itinerant well was first opened by Moses striking the rock with his staff at Horeb, but then the well provided water through song and did not remain at Horeb but became a rolling rock accompanying the traveling pilgrims to provide fresh water for the people and their cattle and sheep. Miriam's song in service to her people opens the well again and again.

"Miriam's Well" also made the desert bloom with green pastures and beautifully scented flowers. So in addition to being the one to inspire celebration at the moment of freedom through song and dance, Miriam is also the one to provide her people with a source of refreshment in the desert heat and dryness. So long as she lived, there was a fountain of living water to sustain the people. Of course, a well provides physical nourishment and also cleansing, but it is also a source and symbol of spiritual nourishment and cleansing.

ICON SYMBOLISM: MIRIAM

The quote at the top of the icon, "all the women went out after her with tambourines and dancing," comes from the text of Exodus. Miriam is depicted having just crossed the Sea of Reeds, dancing joyfully out in the desert with her tambourine. On her ankle is a shackle that has been broken to symbolize her freedom from enslavement in Egypt. The frog joins her in the dance as all creation celebrates this moment with her.

THE ARCHETYPE OF THE PROPHET

In his book *The Prophetic Imagination*, theologian Walter Brueggemann writes that the dominant culture, now and in every time, is grossly uncritical, cannot tolerate any fundamental criticism, and will go to great lengths to stop it. It is the role of the Prophet to help "nurture, nourish, and evoke a consciousness and a perception" alternative to the dominant narrative.

The prophetic voice is not aligned with specific issues but helps to reframe the bigger picture of what is at stake and offers a new sense of what might be possible. In this way, the Prophet is closely connected to the Visionary in this imagining of something new. The Prophet helps us to imagine the world as it might be and how we can get from here to there, and it reminds us that we are bound up with one another. The prophetic voice comes to remind us of the call to solidarity with those who are in need and to remember that our own liberation is intimately entwined with the liberation of the whole human community and the whole natural world.

Prophets tend to emerge in times of chaos and change. Walter Brueggemann describes the necessity of the language of lament, which cries out that things are not as they should be. These powerful cries, found throughout the Hebrew and Christian scriptures, help to name the injustice and break it open.

The true Prophet speaks on behalf of the sender, the Holy Spirit. The journey of the Prophet is to tell the truth no matter the consequences, to stand up to the dominant culture, and to offer an alternative way. The Prophet is not responsible for the outcome and how the words are received. She or he may never see the results of her or his actions, so patience and conviction are required.

Speaking truth can lead to rejection by one's tribe whether family, friends, community, or the wider culture. Jesus was a prophet and was executed for his words and actions. So was Martin Luther King Jr. Once the truth is told, the tribe can either break out of the collective lie they have been living in or continue to live in fear and denial and perpetuate the lie. Most often the tribe acts to protect the dominant mindset and cultural patterns and behaviors. The Prophet is the one who must speak the truth at any cost.

THE SHADOW SIDE OF THE PROPHET
The shadow Prophet can use his or her insight for selfish purposes or to manipulate others. The Prophet must learn discernment about how to voice their message as they can alienate themselves from the community. Alternately, the Prophet emerges in shadow form when he or she varnishes the truth or tries to soften it to reduce risk of rejection.

The Prophet can also easily become overwhelmed by the immense needs of the world. Prophets may feel guilty for taking time off and be at risk of burnout. We find this phenomenon with so many people working in social justice ministry or pastoral care. Prophets must have a healthy sense of humility and focus only on what is theirs to take on in order to sustain the passion and work.

· ·

JESUS AND THE PROPHET ARCHETYPE: "I WAS NAKED AND YOU CLOTHED ME"
REFLECTION BY JOHN VALTERS PAINTNER

When the Son of Man comes in his glory, and all the angels with him, then he will sit on the throne of his glory. All the nations will be gathered before him, and he will separate people one from another as a shepherd separates the sheep from the goats.

—Matthew 25:31–46

Begin by reading the whole scripture passage as indicated and then pray with the excerpt in a contemplative way such as lectio divina (see guidelines in the appendix).

Jesus offered a series of parables about the choices people make and their consequences. In "The Faithful or Unfaithful Servant," one servant is responsible during the master's absence while the other is abusive and neglectful while the master is away. In "The Ten Virgins," half of them showed foresight and brought extra oil for their lambs, but the others found themselves unprepared for the bridegroom's long delay and so were left out of the celebration. And in the parable of "The Talents," two industrious servants double the money left in their care, but the third servant buried the money and therefore incurred the very wrath of the master whom he had feared. Following these Jesus speaks plainly about the final judgment.

He describes the "Son of Man" coming in glory and sitting upon a throne. All the people are separated, the sheep from the goats. The sheep are rewarded for the good deeds they did for him: giving food to the hungry, drink to the thirsty, clothing to the naked, care to the ill, and hospitality to the imprisoned. When the goats complain that they never saw him to do these things, they are reminded of all the times they failed to do good for the least among them.

What ties these stories together is that what one says or claims to believe is not as important as one's actions. It is not enough to call oneself "righteous"; one must *act* righteously.

God's judgment is very black and white in this passage. One either did or did not do these things. And the consequences are severely different for the two groups. It is a harsh punishment, to be sure. But Jesus is not telling this story to predict the future. He is trying to warn the people in time so they might change their thinking and their behavior.

Like the prophets of the Hebrew scriptures, Jesus is giving a "Speech of Judgment." He is naming the accused, reading the charges, and warning of possible verdicts for their actions.

THE PRACTICE OF SABBATH AS RESISTANCE

Last year I read Walter Brueggemann's book *Sabbath as Resistance* and was deeply moved by the power in less than a hundred pages of text.[1] Brueggemann describes the sabbath as a practice of both resistance and alternative.

He writes that the practice of sabbath emerges from the Exodus story, where the Israelites are freed from the relentless labor and productivity of the Pharaoh system in which the people are enslaved and full of the anxiety that deprivation brings. YHWH enters in and liberates them from this exhaustion, commanding that they take rest each week. It may be hard to imagine, but when the Sabbath was given as commandment and covenant, it was a radically new idea. Sabbath practice continued to be a source of misunderstanding and persecution for the descendants of the former slaves throughout biblical times and beyond. And yet it was a foundational practice that held the community together from the exile experience until today.

We essentially live in this self-made, insatiable Pharaoh system again. So weary are we, so burdened by consumer debt, working long hours with very little time off. So many take pride in wearing the badge of "busy." So many are stretched thin to the very edges of their resources.

When we practice Sabbath, we are making a visible statement that our lives are not defined by this. It requires a community to support us.

Brueggemann writes:

> Into this system of hopeless weariness erupts the God of the burning bush (Ex 3:1–6). That God heard the despairing fatigue of the slaves (2:23–25), resolved to liberate the slave company of Israel from that exploitative system (3:7–9) and recruited Moses for the human task of emancipation (3:10). The reason Miriam and the other women can sing and dance at the end of the exodus narrative is the emergence of a new social reality in which the life of the Israelite economy is no longer determined and compelled by the insatiable production quotas of Egypt and its gods (15:20–21).[2]

At the heart of this relationship is a God who celebrates the gift of rest. Brueggemann says we are so beholden to "accomplishing and achieving and possessing" that we refuse the gift given to us.

The Israelites, and we ourselves, must leave Egypt and our enslavement to be able to dance and sing in freedom. Dance is a celebratory act that is not "productive" but restorative. When we don't allow ourselves the gift of sabbath rest, we deny the foundational joy that is our birthright as children of God. To dance in freedom is a prophetic act.

We are called to regularly cease, to trust the world will continue on without us, and to know this embodiment of grace and gift as a revolutionary act. Nothing else needs to be done.

I invite you in the coming days to claim the Sabbath for yourself. The essential element is a commitment to rest and to lay aside work and worry. I highly recommend a technology sabbath as a part of this. Dare to see if the world comes apart if you don't check e-mail for a day. Give yourself the gift of things that are truly restorative—some time spent in silence, a delicious meal shared with a friend or partner, a long walk in a beautiful place. Sabbath-keeping is an embodiment of our faith that there is something deeper at work in the world than the machinations of the power structure.

MEDITATION: INVITING YOUR INNER PROPHET

Find a comfortable position and begin by deepening your breath, letting your inhale and exhale be long and slow. Rest into this rhythm for a few moments as you intentionally draw your energy inward to a still point within. Let yourself savor this space of not doing, of simply resting into the extravagant grace of being. Trust that this is enough for this moment in time. Pause as long as you need to.

From this still center, invite Miriam to become present with you here. See how she appears before you. Welcome her into this space. See the Spirit embrace you both as presence and one who breathes new life into each moment. Ask Miriam and the Spirit to show you your inner Prophet. See how she or he is revealed.

As your Prophet steps forward allow some time to be together; get to know this inner archetype and what he or she has come to show you. What is the truth that must be spoken? Which are the cultural boundaries that leave you feeling trapped that the Prophet can help you to dismantle or challenge? What do you fear losing in the process?

Listen to these words that have been attributed to another great prophet, the archbishop and martyr Óscar Romero who lived in El Salvador, challenging the status quo, a decision that eventually led to his death:

> It helps now and then to step back and take a long view.
> The Kingdom is not only beyond our efforts, it is beyond our vision.
> We accomplish in our lifetime only a fraction of the magnificent enterprise that is God's work.
> Nothing we do is complete, which is another way of saying that the kingdom always lies beyond us.
> No statement says all that could be said.
> No prayer fully expresses our faith.
>
> No confession brings perfection, no pastoral visit brings wholeness.
> No program accomplishes the Church's mission.
> No set of goals and objectives include everything.
>
> This is what we are about.
>
> We plant the seeds that one day will grow.
>
> We water the seeds already planted knowing that they hold future promise.
> We lay foundations that will need further development.
> We provide yeast that produces effects far beyond our capabilities.

> We cannot do everything, and there is a sense of libera-
> tion in realizing this.
> This enables us to do something, and to do it very well.
> It may be incomplete, but it is a beginning, a step along
> the way, an opportunity for the Lord's grace to enter
> and do the rest.
> We may never see the end results, but that is the differ-
> ence between the master builder and the worker.
>
> We are workers, not master builders, ministers, not mes-
> siahs. We are prophets of a future not our own.[3]

Rest into this assurance that our words and work in the world matters, even when we do not see the fruits. Ask Miriam, the Spirit, and your inner Prophet for any wisdom needed to speak your truth. See if there might be a gift offered and receive it. To close this time of meditation notice if your body wants to move into a gesture to embody this prayer.

Let your breath bring you gently back to the room and allow a few minutes to journal any insights or new awareness you had during the meditation.

MANDALA EXPLORATION: SAND ART MANDALAS
For this exploration, you will need to purchase some different col-ors of sand in a craft shop. These often come in multi-packs. Have a round bowl handy as well, preferably wide and flat. A plate would work as well. Also have something to scoop out the sand in small amounts, like a small spoon.

Begin with some centering, finding a way within. Invite your inner Prophet to be with you. Remember Miriam dancing there on the sand in celebration of her freedom. Ask for the grace you desire during this time of prayer.

When you feel ready, notice which color of sand you feel drawn to begin working with. Use the spoon or your fingers to gather a small amount and spread it on the bowl or plate. Keep going in this way, staying connected to your intuition and allowing the image to unfold. When you notice your thoughts rising up and distracting you, gently let them go and return to the invitation of this moment.

Let yourself have some time to explore with the colors of sand, arranging them, designing them, swirling them, playing with them with your fingers.

When you feel ready to finish, sit for a few moments of silence gazing at what has emerged. You might want to record this mandala with your camera. The Tibetan Buddhists have a practice of making intricate and beautiful sand mandalas, and then when done, they blow the sand away as an act of non-attachment. You might consider how you feel called by this art that has emerged from you.

FOR REFLECTION

- What about Miriam's story most inspires or energizes you? Where do you feel the strongest connection or disconnection?
- Where do you feel the prophetic call most strongly in your own life?
- How might you practice sabbath as an act of holy resistance?
- What did the visual art exploration experience reveal to you?

CLOSING BLESSING

I wrote this poem inspired by imagining this moment of crossing the sea and then feeling the incredible urge to dance in absolute joy at freedom. I am so moved to think that Miriam brought her

tambourine with her in departing Egypt, knowing she would want
it soon in celebration.

Miriam on the Shores

All the women went out after her with tambourines and with dancing.

—*Exodus* 15:20

Her skirt hangs heavy with seawater,
staccato breath after running from death.
She can still feel soldiers reaching out
to seize her blouse before the waves caved in.

Collapsing on dry earth for a moment,
the impulse to dance begins in her feet,
spreads slowly upwards like a flock of starlings
rising toward a dawn-lit sky.

So many dances in secret before,
night-stolen movements after exhausting days
heaving stones and harvest.

She finds herself now upright, weeping.
To stand here, face to the sun,
feeling an irrepressible desire to
spin
. . . tumble
sashay
. . . turn
shake
. . . twirl.

Savoring freedom with her limbs
as if it were a physical presence
like a fierce wind or the breath of labor,
shackles slipping off slowly.

She couldn't help but dance.
The story says she picked up her tambourine,
which means she had packed it among the essentials.
In fleeing for her life, she knew this would be necessary.

How many of us still live enslaved in Egypt, beholden and weary?
Do you have the courage to run across the sea parted just now for you?
Will you carry your musical instrument and dance right there on the
   shores?

May you discover your own freedom, leaving behind the exhaustion of anxiety and worry and setting aside the heavy tasks
for a while to know the grace of rest. May you dance freely and
with abandon, celebrating every moment when God calls you
into liberation.

MAY WHAT I DO FLOW FROM ME LIKE A RIVER

RAINER MARIA RILKE

Rainer Maria Rilke: The Artist

· ·

INTRODUCTION TO RAINER MARIA RILKE

May what I do flow from me like a river, no forcing and no holding back.
—Rainer Maria Rilke

Rainer Maria Rilke (1875–1926) is perhaps an unlikely candidate at first glance to join this circle of monks and mystics. He was undeniably opposed to the institutional church; he rejected dogma and what he considered to be second-hand experience of God. On his first visit to a Russian monastery in his twenties, however, he fell in love with the spirituality there, the atmosphere, the reverence, which led him to write one of his first books of poetry *The Book of Hours*, inspired by monastic tradition.

His poems in that book reflect the longings of an imagined monk. But even beyond that initial book, Rainer's poems continued to be suffused with a desire to grow in intimacy with the sacred dimension of the world. He also took his life as poet and artist very seriously; through some of his eleven thousand letters, as well as several books of poems, we have a window into great wisdom for the creative life. He believed in art as a "cosmic, creative, transforming force" and invited us to consider it no less than this.

In *Letters to a Young Poet*, Rainer writes:

> There is only one way: Go within. Search for the cause,
> find the impetus that bids you write. Put it to this test:
> Does it stretch out its roots in the deepest place of your
> heart? Can you avow that you would die if you were
> forbidden to write? Above all, in the most silent hour
> of your night, ask yourself this: Must I write? Dig deep
> into yourself for a true answer. And if it should ring its
> assent, if you can confidently meet this serious question
> with a simple, "I must," then build your life upon it. It
> has become your necessity. Your life, in even the most
> mundane and least significant hour, must become a sign,
> a testimony to this urge.[1]

Rainer is addressing this to a writer, defining what is needed for
full commitment to the creative life. You could substitute the
word "write" with create, paint, dance, garden, cook, love well, or
any other creative endeavor and then read the words again and
see what they stir. These are strong words, with perhaps a hint
of the Warrior at play setting those boundaries. You might pause
here for a moment and reflect with Rainer. Must you create? Do
you experience a compelling need to express your deep desires? If
so, how do you build your life in such a way as to support this?

Describe a perfect day in your life and everything that would be
included from waking to sleeping, the setting, the company, and
the activities. Then consider a real day in your life. How might
you bring some of those elements into the messiness of things?
What are the rhythms and commitments that would support your
creative expression? How might you begin to bring some of these
patterns into your days?

Rainer loved mystery and could see how art, poetry, and prayer
could lead one into a contemplation of the great questions of life,
without needing to grasp at an answer but to let them unfold and

ripen organically. He uses the metaphor of ripening several times both for the individual and for God. This process of *becoming* was central to Rainer's understanding of what it meant to be a poet and artist in life. He doesn't offer us certainty, only the voice of encounter and intimacy, of longing and desire. His well-known quote about learning to love and "live the questions" speaks to this. Searching for answers is at cross-purposes with the creative life; instead, both trust and patience need to be cultivated. Art helps us hold the tensions of paradox and allows us to express the often-felt ambiguity of life.

He also had sage advice about how to be with the difficult periods of our lives. I have often privately called him the patron saint of darkness because he had a way of honoring the dark periods as the fertile ground from which life and creative impulse emerges. "You darkness, that I come from" is the first line of one of his poems, ending with "I have faith in nights." We live in a culture that reverences the energy of spring and summer, the perpetual blossoming and fruitfulness that is impossible to sustain. If we tend to the rhythms of nature, we see that autumn and winter are essential to cycles of growth. Winter's darkness brings hidden gifts.

Rainer trusted the difficulties of the emotional life as a process of slow revelation:

> You must not be frightened . . . when a sadness arises within you of such magnitude as you have never experienced, or when a restlessness overshadows all you do, like light and the shadow of clouds gliding over your hand. You must believe that something is happening to you, that life has not forgotten you, that it holds you in its hand. It shall not let you fall.[2]

I love this image of allowing our sadness to have room within us and the image of all of our deep shadow places and wounds as crying out for support and welcome. If we embrace this perspective then perhaps we can walk into those times of unknowing or self-doubt and see these experiences as offering us wisdom of another kind.

In another letter he describes art as the result of walking mindfully through the experiences of life, welcoming in all that they bring and not denying anything that wants to move through us. Essentially he saw our call in life as simply this: to experience our own unique life with all of its shadows and brilliance as intimately as possible and not to shut out anything just because we deem it too difficult. This is where we discover our own special gift to the world, by allowing all of life to move through us, learning to trust in the process. In his mystical vision, everything belongs, to use a phrase from Richard Rohr. Art calls us to enter into the whole spectrum of life and discover there the inspiration to create.

Rainer read texts about mysticism and mystical experience avidly as he himself tried to express this longing in verse. In another of his letters he writes, "This world, seen no longer with the eyes of men, but in the angel, is perhaps my real task."[3]

To see the world from another perspective can be viewed as one of the tasks of an Artist. To reveal to us the hidden dimension, the poet Gerard Manley Hopkins coined the word *inscape* to describe this inner landscape of objects. It honors the sacred dimension of all of life. In this way Rainer was thoroughly monastic as we remember that St. Benedict asks that we treat the kitchen utensils as sacred as the items on the altar.

He also invites us to cooperate with the elemental forces of the world, "to rise up rooted like trees." Rather than bracing ourselves against the elements and what they might bring, he asks us to yield to the currents: "May what I do flow from me like a river."[4] This organic quality of unfolding was essential to living as an Artist. He sees the rhythms of tides and moon phases as a mirror of our own inner rhythms. The less we resist, the more energy we have for our creative work.

And perhaps as a final word from Rilke, for those of us afraid we have missed our opportunity to live a life of beauty and passion, of poetry and creativity:

> It is not too late
> to dive into your increasing depths
> where life calmly gives out its own secret.[5]

Sometimes we may fear that the time has passed when we could live out our deepest creative dream, but Rainer assures us this is never so. The invitation continues to be extended if you would only say yes.

ICON SYMBOLISM: RAINER MARIA RILKE

The quote on the icon, "may what I do flow from me like a river," comes from a poem that is part of Rainer's collection inspired by his time spent in a Russian monastery, which is also depicted in the icon background. The sun is setting to represent dusk, one of the great hinges of the day when monks gather for prayer.

He holds a quill in his hand because poetry was so much his lifeblood, and a swan swims in the foreground, inspired by another one of my favorite poems of his, "The Swan."

THE ARCHETYPE OF THE ARTIST

Rainer Maria Rilke expressed himself as an artist mostly in poetry and nonfiction writing. The Artist is the part of ourselves that seeks beauty, not just of transcendent moments but of the most ordinary and everyday. Entering into the creative act calls us to make space for the new things being birthed within our very souls by God, the great Artist.

If we explore different religious traditions across time, we find again and again stories of God as Creator of the world and the universe. God is the Sacred Source of all that is alive and pulsing around us, including our own bodies. The Creative Spirit is at work in our lives, moving us toward new possibilities.

Each of us has an inner Artist, the one within us who creates anew and brings things to life. The Artist takes the materials of life and makes something beautiful from them. Even in the midst of pain and suffering, the Artist can craft meaning.

The main tool of the Artist is the imagination, which helps us to find meaning even in the depths of struggle and sorrow. We can begin to imagine a new way of understanding our stories, one that brings beauty to the world. The ultimate artwork is our daily lives. Creating our lives means to give honor to all of our experiences as the material out of which the artwork of our lives is created. We do not need to be a painter or writer or dancer to be an artist. We need to simply follow the impulse we all have to create beauty and meaning. We come to recognize that we participate in creating the world by how we live and by the choices we make.

I love the definition of the Artist as one who creates out of the materials given—not out of what we imagine would be the perfect scenario of time, space, and tools but right in the midst of what life brings. That is where our creativity arises.

The Artist pushes us out of inauthentic roles to claim our true identities, knowing that this may cost us financial security or even friendships. The Artist feels a profound sense of call or vocation in the world, which we come to know by paying attention to and honoring what we are most passionate about. If we all lived from this call, we would create a better world together. When the Artist archetype is active in our lives we are conscious of a sense of purpose and responsibility for a vision for our lives.

Creativity is a union of both hard work and the experience of inspiration. It calls for both activity and surrender. We often need discipline to show up at the blank page or canvas, onto the yoga mat or meditation cushion, or onto the dance floor. But once we are there we need to release our desire to control the process and outcome and give ourselves over to it.

THE SHADOW SIDE OF THE ARTIST

In Julia Cameron's book *The Artist's Way*, she describes one manifestation of the shadow Artist as when we support the creativity of others as a substitute for our own creative life. This may come in many forms, such as when you support others to live to their full potential but neglect your own desires, not leaving any space or time for your own creative nourishment. The shadow also appears when we never sit down to actually write or paint because we are always waiting for the open space in our lives that never arrives and can only be claimed.

Another aspect of the Artist's shadow is workaholism. Those of us deeply in touch with our creative inspiration may get overwhelmed at times by the sheer volume of ideas. Often the Artist at work can move into a creative zone and forget the needs of the body. I know as a writer I can write for hours at a time, never remembering to eat or stretch without active reminders to myself.

If we create purely for reward or recognition rather than as an authentic expression of what is moving within us, we also tap into the shadow Artist. Creating requires that we release our investment in the outcome and response to our work.

The inner critic can often become entwined with the shadow Artist who never completes a work or shares it for fear of imperfection or criticism. This is where the Fool can be a helpful ally, willing to appear foolish for the sake of offering one's gifts.

. . . .

JESUS AND THE ARTIST ARCHETYPE: JESUS WRITES IN THE SAND
REFLECTION BY JOHN VALTERS PAINTNER

Jesus bent down and wrote with his finger on the ground. When they kept on questioning him, he straightened up and said to them, "Let anyone among you who is without sin be the first to throw a stone at her." And once again he bent down and wrote on the ground.

—John 8:3–11

Begin by reading the whole scripture passage as indicated, and then pray with the excerpt in a contemplative way such as lectio divina (see guidelines in the appendix).

This story begins calmly enough. Jesus goes to the Mount of Olives early in the morning and begins preaching to the crowds that flock to him.

Suddenly, Jesus is confronted with a dilemma meant to trap him in a no-win situation. An adulterous woman (assuming the scribes and Pharisees are telling the truth; her "partner in sin" is neither present nor mentioned) is placed in the middle of the crowd of people who have come to hear Jesus. The accusers demand that Jesus be the arbitrator, but they lay out the very specific verdict that must be carried out according to Mosaic Law. They believe it is a black and white issue. If A happened, B must follow. There is no room for interpretation in their eyes.

But Jesus does not fall for their trap. He refuses to let logic of the accusers rule the day when a human life is on the line. Instead, Jesus' response is to stop and write.

We are never told what it is that Jesus writes or draws on the ground with his finger. Some believe it was the sins of the accusers, presumably sins that also carried a mandatory death sentence according to the strict reading of the Law. Maybe Jesus is simply stalling for time. We simply can't know.

What we do know is that Jesus used a creative way of thinking to solve the problem. Part of his solution is the very time it takes to create whatever he is drawing. Jesus puts the brakes on the rush to judgment and, worse still, the rush to punish. Jesus takes the time to think "outside the box" to avoid the trap and to save the woman's life.

But Jesus does more than save her life; he gives her the possibility of a whole new life. We don't know what happened to this woman (she is not Mary of Magdalene, as has been wrongly interpreted throughout the centuries), but we know that she is free to create a new life for herself.

Jesus, the Artist, steps outside the linear and rigid thinking of the Pharisees to create a world in which we can be co-creators.

THE PRACTICE OF BEGINNER'S MIND

Only this time one will not sleep there, one will beg and moan, it doesn't matter;
if then the angel deigns to reappear, it is because you have persuaded him not with
tears but with your humble decision to always begin again: to be a novice!

—*Rainer Maria Rilke*[6]

The Zen tradition offers us the astute practice of beginner's mind, and Benedict describes his *Rule* as a "little Rule for beginners." There are two wonderful little stories from the desert fathers that reflect this wisdom as well:

> Abba Poemen said concerning Abba Pior that every day
> he made a new beginning.

Abba Moses asked Abba Silvanus, "Can a man lay a new foundation every day?" The old man said, "If he works hard he can lay a new foundation at every moment."[7]

The Artist archetype calls us to have beginner's mind, to be open to newness, and to enter into creating as a process of discovery. We create as a way to discover who we are. Creativity is much more enlivening when we embrace it as a process rather than focus on the end product. It becomes a journey of discovery and insight rather than a destination or goal. Allowing ourselves the gift of time to let creativity flow can be a source of great pleasure and delight.

Often the inner critic or judge gets the better of us in our creative process. They seem to trample their way into our thoughts the moment we consider doing something we love. Whether the voices tell you spending time this way is selfish or a waste, they remind you of a time you "failed" or were told by an old art teacher you had no talent, or whatever other story might be simmering inside, know that these voices are a natural part of the creative process. The only thing that makes an Artist different is the willingness to show up to the blank page or the canvas even in the midst of such a cacophony of inner tumult.

We can call in the Fool as an ally to help take ourselves less seriously. If we are beginners, we don't have to worry about getting it "right." We can also call in the Warrior, who is able to witness the self-critical thoughts and create strong inner boundaries, letting the critic know firmly that their services are not needed for this time.

When we cultivate beginner's mind, we can remember we are always beginners on the spiritual path or the creative one. We can risk making "bad" art in service of exploration and practice. We can release the desire for perfection or the old voices echoing within and not invest our entire self-value in each creation. We can discover a newfound freedom from self-doubt and limitation.

MEDITATION: INVITING YOUR INNER ARTIST

Our meditation this time is in part a guided poem-writing exercise inspired by one from poetry therapist John Fox in his book *Finding What You Didn't Lose: Expressing Your Truth and Creativity through Poem-Making.*[8]

Begin by finding a comfortable seated position with pen and paper at hand. You might want to spend five minutes before this meditation simply doing some free-writing, stream of consciousness, to warm up your writing self.

Breathe deeply, allowing your breath to fill you, and then gently release. Spend a few moments tending this life-giving rhythm. Then bring your awareness down to your heart center. Rest here for a moment, soaking in that space of compassion.

Invite in the presence of the poet Rainer Maria Rilke to be with you, and notice how he appears and what form he takes. Then call in the Spirit to guide you, remembering that the root of the word inspiration comes from the Spirit and so we can ask to be infused with the Spirit as the heart of our creative process. Ask them to help reveal your own inner Artist. Allow this image to unfold without trying to force it. See what your Artist looks like, sounds like, and feels like.

Then move into a time of written exploration. I am going to pose a series of questions, and after each one, allow a few moments to write in response. Listen for the initial impulse that stirs in you and engage descriptive language to describe these images, drawing on all of the senses.

I will use the word Artist, but if it is more helpful for you to substitute another word like Poet, Dancer, or Creator please feel free.

- What does your inner Artist look like?
- What does your inner Artist feel like?
- Where was your inner Artist born?
- What does your inner Artist see?
- Where is your inner Artist recognized?
- What does your inner Artist know to be true?
- What does your inner Artist imagine or daydream?
- What kind of place does your inner Artist live?
- What must your inner Artist speak aloud?
- Why does your inner Artist exist?

You can allow some time to read over and shape the words into a poem, but resist the urge to move into your editor stance. Simply receive this as a gift from your inner Artist and savor the images.

It can also be helpful to spend some time writing about the process itself. What did you discover along the way? What resistance came up for you? Where did you experience any ease or flow?

MANDALA EXPLORATION: SAND ART MANDALAS
Just as Jesus wrote in the sand, you are invited into a meditation with sand to explore your inner Artist. You might plan a trip to a nearby beach or shore or perhaps there is a sandbox at a playground. You could also purchase some sand to put into a round bowl at home, similar to those Zen meditation gardens. Keep things simple though.

Begin by finding some stillness through breath and moving your awareness inward. Invite your inner Artist to be present with you in this exploration, and ask for whatever grace you seek during this time of prayer.

Before you begin by drawing in the sand, I will invite you to walk some rounds. In the Irish tradition, walking in a circle in a sunwise direction is an ancient practice of honoring the movements of the cosmos. By walking sunwise, we align ourselves with this cosmic pattern. Make slow circles in the sand around a center point. If you have a bowl of sand, you could simply place it on a small table or the floor and walk around it. Walking the rounds also helps us to release our desire to move in a linear way through the experience, similar to walking a labyrinth.

Walk the rounds in one of the sacred numbers. It might be a single round, three for the Trinity, four for the four elements and seasons, seven for the unity of three and four together, or twelve for the number of disciples. Decide which feels like the invitation today.

As you walk, do so mindfully and prayerfully. Let your breath keep you in the present moment. Much like we drew the circle on the page with intention for our gush art exploration, here we are drawing the circle and container for our space with our bodies.

After completion of the rounds, sit down and allow some deep breaths again. Then using your fingers or hands, simply allow a time of drawing in the sand within the circle that has been created. Do not worry if the sand doesn't hold the shape; this is an exercise in letting go of the outcome.

Just let yourself enter into this time of playful exploration, seeing how your hands want to move through the sand and shape it. When you come to a place of completion, rest for a few moments in silence.

FOR REFLECTION

- What about Rainer's story most inspires or energizes you? Where do you feel the strongest connection or disconnection?
- How does your inner Artist want to be seen in the world? Where do you deny this part of yourself?

- How might you practice beginner's mind as a way of releasing your desire for perfection and accomplishment? What kind of freedom might this offer to you?
- What did the visual art exploration experience reveal to you?

CLOSING BLESSING

My poem offering for you is in a slightly different format than usual. Rather than a story of the monk or mystic or speaking directly in their voice, I offer this piece that feels inspired by Rilke's own insight that the role of an Artist is to see in a different way, which he expressed with this line of poetry: "my looking ripens things." For Rainer, to be an artist or poet or creator demanded that we give ourselves wholly to this task and clear away that which stands in the way. Ultimately, it isn't about just creating poems or paintings but about seeing the world as its own kind of poem or seeing that my inner Artist is bringing me into a more intimate communion with the world around me, and that is her or his deepest purpose for my life, to see beauty all around.

> **This is not a poem**
> but a rain-soaked day keeping me inside
> with you and you loving me like a storm.
>
> This is not a poem but a record of a hundred mornings
> when the sun lifted above the stone hills outside my window.
>
> This is time for boiling water poured into the chipped cup
> holding elderflower, hawthorn, mugwort.
>
> This is not a poem but me standing perfectly still on the edge of the lake
> in autumn, watching a hundred starlings like prayer flags fluttering.
>
> This is my face buried in May's first pink peony,
> petals just now parting, eyes closed, inhaling.

This is not a poem but the field beyond thought and judgment
and the ways I tear myself apart on too many fine days.

This is the place where clocks no longer matter unless
it is the dusty gold watch that belonged to my grandfather.

This is not a poem but me standing desolate in a parade
of white gravestones, when a single bluebird lands and sings.

This is the bunch of Gerbera daisies you handed to me one foggy
February afternoon, pale yellow like the long-forgotten sun.

This is the first bite of bread after too many hungry days,
this is my grandmother whispering her secrets to me after dusk.

This is not a poem but me taking off my clothes
and stepping eagerly into the cold mid-December sea.

This is the silence between breaths and in that stillness
this is me saying yes and yes and yes.

May your inner Artist reveal the beauty of a hundred ordinary moments. May you commit yourself to cultivating this path of vision, and may the world ripen under your gaze.

Hildegard of Bingen: The Visionary

Fire of the Holy Spirit,
life of the life of every creature,
holy are you in giving life to forms.
Rivers spring forth from the waters
earth wears her green vigor.
—Hildegard of Bingen

Hildegard of Bingen (1098–1179) was a twelfth-century Benedictine abbess who in 2012 was canonized as a saint and made a Doctor of the Catholic Church (one of only four women). She was a Visionary leader of extraordinary creative power: a monk, herbal healer, visual artist, musician and composer of chant, preacher, spiritual director, prophet, and poet—the list goes on and on. She lived for eighty-one years with ongoing chronic health conditions and still left us with a tremendous legacy.

One of her great gifts was insight into what she called *viriditas*, or the greening power of God, the life force at work in all of creation. This central creative principle was key for Hildegard in understanding the vibrancy of her soul and her work. *Viriditas* is the force sustaining life each moment, bringing newness to birth. It is a marvelous image of the divine power continuously at work in the world, juicy and fecund.

We often experience our life as a kind of wandering through the desert, experiencing the spareness of the landscape. But there is another side to the desert. The prophet Isaiah writes that "the wilderness and the dry land shall be glad, the desert shall rejoice and blossom; like the crocus it shall blossom abundantly, and rejoice with joy and singing" (Is 35:1–2).

This abundant blossoming is the provenance of *viriditas*. We are called to wander through the desert tending to the abundant gifts of *viriditas*, the creative life-giving force at the heart of everything alive. Hildegard's wisdom is for living a life that is fruitful and green and overflowing with verdancy. She calls us to look for fecundity in barren places.

She was my doorway into the Benedictine life. While in graduate school I was studying for my "History of Christian Spirituality" comprehensive examination and actually had a slight disdain for those ancient monks. My spirituality up until that point had been quite infused by the Ignatian vision of service and working for justice. I was turned off by the body-denying practices of monasticism (at least in some of its earlier forms) and wondered how those who chose a cloistered life could truly be engaged with the suffering of the world.

Of course, I hadn't yet seen how my own life and spiritual practice up until that point had actually been thoroughly monastic already, with my love of silence, my longing for sacred rhythms, my love of books and art, and my ability to see God pulsing in all of creation and through the seasons. Art and nature had been my two primary places of revelation for most of my life. Then I began reading Hildegard. I had to read her for those exams, but I was captivated by her because of the sheer brilliance and expansiveness of her life. Here was a twelfth-century woman who was abundantly talented and also courageous enough to challenge the hierarchy of the church of her day, telling them if God had to send a woman to deliver his message, things must have gotten really bad. My feminist heart cringed, but I could see the rhetorical device between the lines and the way she was able to shame those in power using their own stereotypes and limited vision against them. I don't believe for a minute Hildegard thought she was any less capable because she was a woman. Her letters demonstrate all the fierce ways she fought passionately for the things she believed in.

What I grew to love about her was her complexity. Certainly I felt a kinship to her because of her love of the arts—she believed that singing chant was the most important practice of her community—and her ability to see God in nature.

I also loved that while I identified fully with her vision of art and creation as essential sources of revelation of the divine nature, I found myself challenged by her apocalyptic mindset. She believed in the end times and the fiery wrath of God. She had powerful visions that showed what was to come. She lived in a very different age and some elements of her theology made me entirely uncomfortable. But I grew to love that she was complex enough for me to discover in her a kindred spirit and a strange bedfellow all at once.

The more I studied her, the more I wanted to know about this Benedictine tradition she was so steeped in. I consider her in many ways the patron saint of my journey toward becoming a Benedictine Oblate. Her complexity calls me to wrestle with the things I both love and hate. For me, one of the hallmarks of the Benedictine journey is in what I call "radical hospitality"—the welcoming in of all that is uncomfortable (especially within ourselves) as a primary place of God's revelation.

In early autumn 2013, I had the great privilege of leading a pilgrimage to the landscape of Hildegard of Bingen with my dear teaching partner Betsey Beckman and the wonderful folks at Spiritual Directors International.

I had been to that place of lush greenness once before the previous autumn, and on that pilgrimage I discovered *viriditas* in a new way. While I expected to see this greening power alive in the vineyards draping the hills, in the beauty of the Rhine River flowing through the valley like a glorious vein of life, and in the forested hill of Disibodenberg where Hildegard spent much of her early life, what I received as gift was the greening that came alive for me in the community gathered.

The "greening" of the area where she lived is powerful. She was a landscape mystic, meaning that the geography of her world was a means of ongoing revelation into the nature of God. Gazing out over the shimmering autumn gold of the vineyards beyond St. Hildegard's monastery in Rudesheim, Germany, I felt this sense of deep surrender where that porous line between me and the earth seemed to fade. I let that green energy of the earth rise up and embrace me in ways I hadn't previously experienced. I imagined Hildegard breathing this vision in and out. I felt the pulsing of God's creative power through me in new ways. The sacred is the quickening force animating and enlivening the whole world, including our own beings. The flourishing of the world around Hildegard was the impetus for her to embrace her inner flourishing.

I consider Hildegard one of my spiritual directors, her voice providing guidance to me across the centuries. We know much about her practical wisdom through the letters she wrote to a variety of people in response to their requests for care. I like to think of this as an early form of epistolary spiritual direction. In her advice to another abbess she writes, "A person who toils more than her body can bear is rendered useless in her spirit by ill-judged roil and abstinence. Living hopelessly and joylessly, that person's sense often fails."

The key to creative flourishing for Hildegard is cultivating moderation and balance. The virtue of *discretio* is about discerning the right path and not being overburdened or overworked so that we are stretched too thin and joy is lost. Our greening is lost when we lose sight of the call to stillness and presence.

ICON SYMBOLISM: HILDEGARD OF BINGEN

Hildegard is wearing a green robe for the *viriditas* she saw so profusely in the world. She is barefoot in the grass and among trees, the place for her of divine revelation. She holds a crozier, which is the sign of her rank as abbess and leader of her community. In her other hand she holds a feather, alluding to this image in the quote above. To be a "feather on the breath of God" means to yield oneself to the divine current, to let yourself be carried by grace rather than force of personal will. Above her are the flames of the "living light"—one of her main images for God and what initiated her visions. In one of her self-portraits she is depicted as receiving these rays of light as she writes, an acknowledgment of the divine inspiration of her writings.

As a Visionary, Hildegard was guided by this living light to open herself to see the world in new ways.

THE ARCHETYPE OF THE VISIONARY

> *The Spirit of God is a life that bestows life, root of the world-tree and wind in its boughs. Scrubbing out sins, she rubs oil into wounds. She is glistening life alluring all praise, all-awakening, all-resurrecting.*
>
> —Hildegard of Bingen[1]

Hildegard had many powerful visions in her life that became the source for three volumes on theology. She offers us fresh images of the divine presence in the world and calls us to see things anew. Hildegard embodied the archetype of the Visionary, the one within each of us who allows us to see beyond the horizons of our own limited lives and perspective.

The Visionary is the part of ourselves that knows we have something holy to birth into the world and can see past our self-imposed limitations and expectations to a reality more brilliant and alluring than we are often ready to acknowledge.

This passage from the prophet Isaiah is one of my favorites and speaks to the heart of the Visionary:

> Now I am revealing new things to you
> Things hidden and unknown to you
> Created just now, this very moment.
> Of these things you have heard nothing until now.
> So that you cannot say, Oh yes, I knew this." (Is 48:6–7, *Jerusalem Bible*)

Visionaries trust in this divine unfolding. They know themselves as collaborators with the creative upwelling already at work in the world. They can see the shape of possibilities by paying attention to night dreams and synchronicities. Visionaries often see images and symbols that arise and perhaps do not make sense at first, but they allow themselves to be carried like feathers on the breath of God or to flow on the currents of divine love.

Intuition is another honored guide of Visionaries, and they have learned to trust inner knowings, leanings, and nudges as coming from a divine source beyond personal knowledge. They are the midwives of what is possible, opening the way for the future to enter long before it is born. They see great promise for humanity and the world, even in the face of the daily news.

The Visionary is called to offer these insights on behalf of the wider community and is tested with others who know us. We each can call upon this part of ourselves and then share the possibilities we see on the horizon. The Visionary is an edge-dweller, not satisfied with the status quo.

THE SHADOW SIDE OF THE VISIONARY

The Visionary in its shadow form misses the grace of *this* moment, always living for the future and in a state of perpetual discontent for the present not living up to possibilities imagined. They are always feeling anxious and helpless about the future, or they have the visions but not the discipline to enact them and bring them into being.

Not all visions are holy; some are rooted in ego desires and the will to control. That is why they must always be brought into community, first perhaps with a spiritual director or wise guide who can help us to test whether they are life-giving or ultimately destructive.

The shadow Visionary sometimes sabotages the possibilities being offered or adapts a message to make it more acceptable to society or uses it for financial gain.

JESUS AND THE VISIONARY ARCHETYPE: THE TRANSFIGURATION
REFLECTION BY JOHN VALTERS PAINTNER

Six days later, Jesus took with him Peter and James and his brother John and led them up a high mountain, by themselves. And he was transfigured before them, and his face shone like the sun, and his clothes became dazzling white. Suddenly there appeared to them Moses and Elijah, talking with him.

—Matthew 17:1–8

Begin by reading the whole scripture passage as indicated and then pray with the excerpt in a contemplative way such as lectio divina (see guidelines in the appendix).

Surprisingly, this major revelation about Jesus' true identity does not come at the end of Matthew's gospel but near the middle.

Jesus has been rejected as a prophet in his home town of Nazareth, and his cousin, John the Baptist, has been put to death. But rather than withdraw from public life, Jesus performs several miracles witnessed by the apostles. He feeds the thousands before walking on water. Jesus heals many people, including the Canaanite woman of great faith. In response to this string of miracles, the Pharisees and Sadducees criticize Jesus for not following every minute rule of the Law. Not wanting to recognize Jesus' authority, they nitpick his apostles.

The Pharisees and Sadducees go so far as to demand a sign from Jesus. In contrast, Peter has just confessed his belief in Jesus as the Messiah without the need of further proof. Jesus goes on to discuss the price of true discipleship before taking a select few with him to the mountaintop. There, Jesus is transformed before their eyes, and they see him in his full glory. It may take them some time to completely process this new experience, but they have been shown all they need to see.

The vision that Jesus usually presents to the disciples and the crowds is a verbal one. Here, Jesus physically shows some of the apostles the kingdom of God. Jesus shines with light, a recurring image of God in the Old Testament. Even the great religious figures of the Hebrew scriptures, Moses and Elijah, appear beside him. Past and present, with a glimpse of the further to come, are merged in the eternal now. And in a repeat of Jesus' Baptism, a voice from the heavens proclaims Jesus the beloved Son with whom God is well pleased.

At a loss for how to respond to this vision, this revelation, Peter suggests erecting tents. Like Hildegard commissioning a painter to memorialize her visions, Peter wants to create at least a temporary monument to this event.

But Jesus declines and calls for the disciples to stand beside him and be not afraid. He is asking the disciples to be truly present to the moment. They are then able to see Jesus in his true form, a vision beyond the expectations and realities of the everyday.

THE PRACTICE OF YIELDING

When I introduce people to the contemplative practice of photography, the first principle I explore is that of shifting our perspective from "taking photos" to "receiving images as gifts." So much of our language in photography is about "taking," "capturing," and "shooting," which reflects a culture that wants to seize control of everything and commodify it. If you have ever found yourself in a situation where you were taking as many photos as possible of an event or experience as a way of capturing it to share, you were caught up in this energy.

The contemplative path calls us to a different perspective. Rather than taking what we want or expect, we are called to breathe deeply and approach the world from a perspective of spaciousness and anticipation. The Visionary calls us to see the world as full of holy surprise and divine unfolding. Contemplative practices that encourage softening our grasp open us up to visions we couldn't have seen otherwise.

In the Yoga Sutras there is a wonderful term: *aparigraha*, which means non-grasping. We share the same principle in Christian monastic tradition, but I appreciate this word as a concrete practice, as a way to approach life around us through a more open-palmed and open-hearted way. You might even try clenching your fist tightly, then breathing deeply and opening your hand into a wide-open palm, and then holding this gesture of receiving. Feel the difference between these two physical postures.

When we approach the world through what we expect to see, often through the lens of cynicism and mistrust or through fear and anxiety, the world is seen as a grey and dim reflection of our hopes.

When we yield our own agendas and release our need to command, excel, seek, and own, we are opened to a very different kind of wisdom in the world. This is the wisdom the Visionary sees. This is what Hildegard of Bingen could perceive beyond the surface of things: she saw the greening power of God suffusing all of life and creation. This came to be a primary principle of discernment—how green was my soul, how green was my community? What was causing dryness and barrenness?

MEDITATION: INVITING YOUR INNER VISIONARY

Begin by allowing some deep breaths, drawing the inhale slowly down into your belly, and letting the exhale be long and slow. As you breathe in, imagine you are welcoming in the presence of the Spirit as guidance, knowing that in the ancient imagination, breath indicated the movement of the Spirit at work. As you breathe out, imagine you are softening any places of grasping. This might be tightness in your muscles creating tension and stiffness. Bring your breath to these places and release the holding as much as possible.

Soften the hard thoughts you may be carrying—worries about the future, planning for the day, writing your to-do list, or holding expectations about what this meditation or experience will or will not bring.

Soften any hardness of heart: the ways you turn on yourself without compassion and others in your life who foster resentment. Just set these aside and open yourself to the infinite compassion of the divine indwelling. Open your heart to receive whatever gift may come in this time of rest and imagining.

Invite in the presence of Hildegard of Bingen. See her surrounded by greenness and inviting you into an experience of the lush possibilities of your life. See her pointing to the Spirit all around who is the guide for whatever visions may come. Let the presence of both of them be with you as you listen.

Notice your body's response to this invitation, and soften anyplace that begins to tighten. Know that you are accompanied in this process by many wise ones.

Continue breathing deeply and holding a very spacious inner awareness. As thoughts arise, simply witness them and let them float past. If a strong feeling arises, breathe into it rather than resisting it, and let it move through your body. Do not hold onto any one thing; thoughts and feelings can flow through like a current of air or a river.

Imagine that you hold out your palms in a position of receiving without any expectation of what will arrive there. You can even hold your hands physically in this posture. If you notice judgments arise or anticipation about what will or won't happen, see if you might breathe into those and let them go.

Stay present to your open palms and any images or symbols that land there. If your mind starts to grasp, breathe again and release. Just stay with the experience as long as you need to until something emerges. If it doesn't seem to make any sense, see if you might simply trust the process and let go of your need to figure out what it means.

Once an image or symbol arises and you have a sense that this might be a gift for you right now, offer it to Hildegard and the

Spirit's wise counsel. See if they have a response; it may not come in words. Ask them for their blessing of this vision and see if it comes.

When you are ready to close the meditation, see if there is a physical gesture for what has arisen in your prayer. Repeat this gesture throughout your day as an embodied expression of this prayer that has arisen in you.

Allow some time to close with written reflection. Make note of anything you noticed in this process of tending to what was unfolding. Honor the symbol or image by writing it down as well. Hold it gently, without the need to figure it out for now.

MANDALA EXPLORATION: NATURE MANDALAS

You are invited to another contemplative walk. Go somewhere like a park or seashore where there will be natural elements available. Invite your inner Visionary to be a part of this exploration; let him or her help you to see differently. Ask for whatever grace you desire to enter into this as a time of prayer.

Become aware of materials along your path that could be used as materials for your own creation—stones, sticks, leaves, and flowers. See if you can use found materials, rather than breaking things off branches or stems. The earth offers up plenty of organic material to the great compost of life.

Let this be a contemplative experience, listening for what objects shimmer for you and seem to hold wisdom or meaning or stories.

Once you have "enough" materials, find a place to pause and enter into a time of creation. Stack stones, arrange leaves, and scatter acorns into a mandala. Create several mandalas or just a single one. See how you feel led.

Release the thinking, judging mind as much as possible. When thoughts do enter in, simply notice them and let them go as you return to your task.

Ask the stones where they want to be laid; have a conversation with the twigs and leaves about how they want to be in relationship to one another. If the whole idea of talking to your materials makes you feel foolish, embrace the foolishness, and remember that this is about prayer and play. Let your Visionary show you the depth of the encounter with creation.

When you have arrived at your "destination" and there is a feeling of satisfaction with what has emerged, simply sit with it for a while. Just notice your own experience. What do you discover as creator? How do you experience this kind of co-creation with the natural world?

You might want to receive this creation with a photo to record it and receive it as gift. Or you might not. Check in to see whether the photo aspect feels too grasping, too much like checking off an assignment or trying to create something permanent, rather than allowing yourself an experience. Trust whatever emerges in response. Thank the materials for their invitation to you to participate with them in creating more beauty.

Then walk away. Practice humility and surrender by knowing that the organic nature of things means that this creation will eventually disintegrate back to the earth, rather than be forever captured in the great halls of a museum.

FOR REFLECTION

- What about Hildegard's story most inspires or energizes you? Where do you feel the strongest connection or disconnection?
- How does *viriditas* come alive in your life?
- How might you practice yielding of your own agenda in life?

- What did the visual art exploration experience reveal to you?

CLOSING BLESSING

To close I share a poem I wrote for Hildegard that celebrates her role as monk, herbalist, and musical composer and is also connected to a story at the end of her life when the church authorities of her time came into dispute with her over a body buried in her abbey's cemetery. The hierarchy believed it was a man who had fallen away from the Church, but she held fast that he had reconciled before his death and so she was unwilling to allow them to dig up his body. In response she was forbidden from singing her beloved Divine Office and from receiving communion.

St. Hildegard Strolls through the Garden

Luminous morning, Hildegard gazes at
the array of blooms, holding in her heart
the young boy with a mysterious rash, the woman

reaching menopause, the newly minted widower,
and the black abbey cat with digestive issues who wandered
in one night and stayed. New complaints arrive each day.

She gathers bunches of dandelions, their yellow
profusion a welcome sight in the monastery garden,
red clover, nettle, fennel, sprigs of parsley to boil later in wine.

She glances to make sure none of her sisters are
peering around pillars, slips off her worn leather shoes
to relish the freshness between her toes,

face upturned to the rising sun, she sings *lucida materia*,
matrix of light, words to the Virgin, makes a mental
note to return to the scriptorium to write that image down.

When the church bells ring for Lauds, she hesitates just a
moment, knowing her morning praise has already begun,
wanting to linger in this space where the dew still clings.

At the end of her life, she met with a terrible obstinacy,
from the hierarchy came a ban on receiving
bread and wine and her cherished singing.

She now clips a single rose, medicine for a broken heart,
which she will sip slowly in tea, along with her favorite spelt
biscuits, and offer some to the widower

grieving for his own lost beloved,
they smile together softly at this act of holy communion
and the music rising among blades of grass.

I wish you many moments of communion with bread and tea
and the music that rises from the earth. May your inner Visionary
continue to invite you deeper into what is yours to see. May you
continue to listen to her or his wisdom and guidance as you await
the holy being birthed within.

Thomas Merton: The Monk

∙ ∙

INTRODUCTION TO THOMAS MERTON

The world and time are the dance of the Lord in emptiness. The silence of the spheres is the music of a wedding feast. The more we persist in misunderstanding the phenomena of life, the more we analyze them out into strange finalities and complex purposes of our own, the more we involve ourselves in sadness, absurdity, and despair.

But it does not matter much, because no despair of ours can alter the reality of things, or stain the joy of the cosmic dance which is always there. Indeed we are in the midst of it, and it is in the midst of us, for it beats in our very blood, whether we want it to or not.

Yet the fact remains that we are invited to forget ourselves on purpose, cast our awful solemnity to the winds and join in the general dance.

—Thomas Merton[1]

This passage is one of my favorites by Thomas Merton (1098–1179) and is part of the inspiration behind the Holy Disorder of Dancing Monks, the name of our contemplative and creative community at Abbey of the Arts, a virtual monastery shepherded by my husband and myself. This image of the cosmic dance, unfolding despite ourselves, brings me joy and reminds me to release the ways in which I struggle against it.

For me, this is the gift of contemplative practice, this reminder that my own grasping at what I think is most essential is so often not. Being a Monk is, of course, one of the archetypes with which I most deeply identify. Perhaps that is because I need it so much. My tendency is to live ten steps ahead of myself with my active mind always trying to figure things out. Thomas Merton had the incredible gift of making much of monastic teaching and the contemplative life accessible to modern ears. A twentieth-century Trappist monk, his writing broke open the treasures of monastic tradition for a whole generation and those who followed. Trappists are part of the Benedictine family, essentially a reform movement that began in the seventeenth century when the abbot of La Trappe monastery in France felt the Cistercians had become too liberal. The reform was a return to simplicity.

I love the way nature was a profound teacher and wisdom guide for Thomas. He experienced all of creation as pointing the way toward our true selves, which is who we were created to be at heart by the divine creative force and not who we imagine ourselves to be with all of our agendas, goals, and strivings. He saw the lakes, the sea, the mountains, trees, and animals as saints because they are so intrinsically themselves. To be a saint means to be fully oneself. These elements of creation do not spin stories that take them away from their true nature. There is so much grace for us to discover in witnessing them, letting their wisdom into our lives. We get to choose whether to be true or false, real or unreal.

Thomas writes, "Forest and field, sun and wind and sky, earth and water, all speak the same silent language, reminding the monk that he is here to develop like the things that grow all around him."[2] The elements of earth, wind, water, and fire all help the Monk cultivate the inner life organically rather than in forced ways. I am reminded here of Rainer Maria Rilke's line, "no forcing and no holding back." Thomas would find in creation the very source of his prayer, describing that as he seeks silence and solitude he discovers that everything he touches is turned into prayer: "The sky is my prayer, the birds are my prayer, the wind in the trees is my prayer, for God is in all."[3] It is this profound insight of God in all that is the central revelation of the contemplative life. Practice awakens us to this reality slowly and allows love to seize us rather than fear or worry.

Perhaps the other most profound of Thomas's quotes for my own life has been this one that he wrote in his book *Conjectures of a Guilty Bystander:* "The rush and pressure of modern life are a form, perhaps the most common form, of its innate violence. To allow oneself to be carried away by a multitude of conflicting concerns, to surrender to too many demands, to commit oneself to too many projects, to want to help everyone in everything is to succumb to violence."[4]

I first read this quote several years ago in a *Yoga Journal* article on the practice of *ahimsa,* or nonviolence. It stunned me because I had never before even considered that the busyness of my life might be a form of violence in which I participate. Thomas is not writing this to corporate culture but to peace activists and other well-meaning folks in the church trying to do good things, too many good things.

While I have always been drawn to the contemplative life, I have never quite looked at busyness in the same way again. I work a lot with people in ministry, mostly training them to use the arts and contemplation in their work and prayer and self-care. When I taught classes in seminaries, I was often shocked and dismayed to see students stretched so far by school demands that there was really no time and space to integrate all the shifts happening in their understanding or to create life-giving patterns for future ministry. It saddens me because seminary is the place where healthy habits and practices for ministry can be set in place. I wish there was more emphasis on self-care and a recognition of the violence we do to ourselves when we, as Thomas says, commit to too many projects and demands. Church culture is just as guilty of this, demanding just as much time and energy as the busy corporate world. In the name of doing good work, we keep going.

And yet faith communities have an opportunity, really a *responsibility*, to be a witness to the world of a genuine alternative way of being. This is one of their prophetic tasks, one that doesn't invest our value solely in what we do and achieve. It is a way of being that embraces the humility to know when we have reached our limits and when we need to say no for the sake of greater life.

Thomas's insight into the violent nature of our doing and busyness led me to an epiphany about the contemplative life. So much has been written about the balance between contemplation and action and how contemplative prayer can renew us to continue the hard path toward justice. To be sure, this is all true, but what I began to see was the contemplative life *itself* as a path of justice, a witness to the world of a way of being that releases the bonds of compulsive doing and resists the violence that busyness can unleash on our bodies, our relationships, and our communities. We began to explore this in the previous chapter in the connection between the Prophet and the practice of sabbath.

Indeed, there are so *many* good things we could do in the world, but investing our energy in the multitude of goods that exist is an enemy of the best, the way that God calls us most deeply to follow—a way that emerges out of who we are and that honors *both* our gifts and our limitations. Maturity in the spiritual life means knowing what we are both called to do and called *not* to do. Self-care means good stewardship of the gifts we have been given and the body that is the vessel that offers them.

Creativity is essential to the world, to imagine new possibilities. Yet so many of us lead lives that are so full there is barely room for God's newness to erupt in us or for us to even recognize those stirrings when they happen. The monastic path offers us guidance in this direction.

ICON SYMBOLISM: THOMAS MERTON

The quote above the icon, "join in the joy of the cosmic dance," comes from the passage by Thomas quoted in the opening section, from the very end of his book *New Seeds of Contemplation*. He is pictured standing in front of Gethsemane Abbey in Kentucky where he made his monastic vows and lived as a monk. There is also a Buddhist stupa to one side as the dialogue between Eastern and Western spiritual traditions became very important to him at the end of his life. He has a camera around his neck because he discovered the joy of photography as a contemplative practice, and he is depicted dancing with the birds and squirrels as nature was essential to him as a place of inspiration and prayer.

THE ARCHETYPE OF THE MONK

The root of the word monk is *monachos*, which means single, as in singular of focus or single-hearted. The Monk seeks to discover the divine presence in everything, every moment, and every person. This is, of course, a lifelong practice and is never "perfected."

The Monk seeks wisdom, knowing this comes through showing up to the struggles of the inner life. Stability and a commitment to staying with our experience is at the core of the monastic life. There is a commitment to be present to the moment and not run away, whether physically or emotionally. The Monk knows that staying with discomfort yields grace and growing freedom.

Connected to this is hospitality and welcoming in the stranger. Monasteries have traditionally been sought out as places of refuge and sanctuary. In medieval Ireland, this was literally true as the laws of the kingdoms did not apply within the monastic complex. So the Monk invites us to let in all that is strange, both within and without, and welcome it as a divine guide.

The Monk treasures reflection and time spent in solitude and silence, knowing that in this time, rich connection to the inner life is fostered and then spills over into connection with the world. In some monastic traditions, there was greater emphasis on the hermit, who retreated out to the wilderness and was then sought out by those desiring wisdom. Other traditions emphasized the communal nature of the monastery and the support needed for the rigor of this life commitment. In Celtic traditions, a monk was expected to have an *anam cara*, or soul friend, with whom he could reveal all the struggles of the soul.

There is a discipline in the monastic life of committing oneself to prayer practices that reminds us of the divine indwelling in each moment and within us. The Monk relishes the gift that this practice brings. These practices also help us to shed our false identities and continually return to the indwelling spark that is our divine nature.

THE SHADOW SIDE OF THE MONK

The shadow Monk can appear in different forms. Isolation is one seduction the Monk brings; sometimes the world of other people can become too much and we can seek solitude not out of desire for union with God, which always brings us to a sense of our deeper connection with humanity, but out of a desire to run away from the messiness of relationship.

The Monk in shadow form also retreats to escape from the world or to detach oneself from worldly concerns. This can arise from a sense of despair over the world's troubles and lead to a sense of giving up. We can justify this by turning to our inner Monk, but in reality, the intention behind it is shadowed. Solitude is always meant to replenish us to return to the world, not escape it. The longer the Monk stays in the cave, the harder it can become to leave it as the pleasures of living in a self-created world can be seductive and more appealing than the flesh and blood world in which we must participate.

The shadow of the Monk can also reveal itself in a desire to stay in the world of ideas and deep thoughts rather than being engaged with the body and the sensual dimensions of the world.

JESUS AND THE MONK ARCHETYPE: "COME REST AWHILE"
REFLECTION BY JOHN VALTERS PAINTNER

The apostles gathered around Jesus, and told him all that they had done and taught. He said to them, "Come away to a deserted place all by yourselves and rest a while."

—Mark 6:30–33

Begin by reading the whole scripture passage as indicated and then pray with the excerpt in a contemplative way such as lectio divina (see guidelines in the appendix).

The Gospel of Mark is a short, quick read. Even so, it is surprising to note how quickly Jesus sends the Twelve out on their own missions.

Mark's is the only synoptic gospel to exclude an infancy narrative. Even the Gospel of John at least includes the preamble about the Word preexisting Jesus. But Mark starts with Jesus' Baptism and moves straight into the call of the disciples. Jesus is even healing the sick and performing miracles by the end of the first chapter. And the miracles keep coming, in quick succession. At the end of chapter 3, Jesus is sending the Twelve out on their first mission before he is confronted, first by the scribes and then his own family.

The pace of Mark's gospel slows a bit with the start of chapter 4 and a series of parables. But soon Jesus is back to performing miracles. First, Jesus calms the sea merely by speaking in a scene meant to invoke the first Creation Myth at the very start of the book of Genesis. Jesus' divine nature is also revealed in the casting out of demons. He is able to cure the afflicted just by the touch of his cloak. Unfortunately, none of this impresses the people of his native Nazareth who reject him.

It is at this point that Jesus sends the Twelve on their first mission (and it's only halfway through the sixth of sixteen chapters). Jesus gives them authority and strict instructions to travel lightly. They work independently from Jesus but in pairs. After working amongst the people they return to Jesus. His first instruction upon their return is to seek solitude in order to recover.

There is a rapid, single-mindedness to Mark's gospel. The focus of Jesus' mission is clear and urgent. However, even Jesus takes time to stop and reflect. The message Jesus seems to be sending is that constant work, even God's work, can be detrimental. There is a time to be with others and a time to be apart. Even ministers need a sabbath. Jesus himself demonstrates the need to be alone on numerous occasions, including the night he is arrested.

THE PRACTICE OF PARADISE

In the Christian tradition, we encounter a vision of paradise as a place of wholeness in the Garden of Eden, the peaceable kingdom of Isaiah, and the heavenly city of the book of Revelation. The reality we encounter in our daily lives feels much different. The news is rife with evidence that we live anyplace but paradise. We are confronted with growing degradation and fragmentation at every turn. And yet, this vision of a place of wholeness can help us inhabit an imaginative space that leads us to work toward the renewal of this world rather than withdrawing in despair.

One of my favorite books on contemplative practice and desert tradition is Douglas E. Christie's *Blue Sapphire of the Mind*. It is dense and best read slowly, so it took me several months to get to the final chapter, but that chapter has had a profound impact on my own perspective. In it he suggests that we must learn to "practice paradise, to learn how to incorporate an awareness of this mysterious reality into the heart of our contemplative practice." Christie describes our "profound and persistent alienation from the world,"[5] which is known theologically as sin, a primordial experience of exile and a profound longing for home. We feel far away from Paradise.

The contemplative tradition offers us great wisdom for the ways we so often strive, grasp for things beyond our reach, live beyond our means, exert great effort to achieve and produce, and live on a seemingly endless treadmill of exertion. Monasticism offers the question of whether it is possible to live a life "free from care" rooted in Jesus' teachings: "Therefore I tell you, do not worry about your life, what you will eat or what you will drink, or about your body, what you will wear. Is not life more than food, and the body than clothing? Look at the birds of the air; they neither sow nor reap nor gather into barns, and yet your heavenly Father feeds them. Are you not of more value than they? And can any of you by worrying add a single hour to your span of life?" (Mt 6:25–27).

This encapsulated exactly what the early monks desired, a life free from the debilitation of anxiety and fear, a life in ever-increasing freedom. The asceticism and profound simplicity of their lives was an attempt to heal this anxiety and learn to grow free of their obsessive attachment to things. They desired a profound freedom from anxiety and to live in the depths of trust in divine abundance and provision. This practice was directed toward the act of recovering paradise in the here and now. The act of freeing ourselves from things leads us to be able to respond to one another without agenda or to think of the other person's usefulness in our lives. Meaning can be found apart from utility.

This practice draws us toward a profound contemplative awareness and affection for all the ordinary moments of life, as the Artist teaches us. We can learn to value the world for itself and not for what it brings us. When anxiety arises, we can call upon our inner Warrior to help us root it out. The monastic way values leisure, rest, play, presence, and time spent doing nothing. It breaks open our conventional categories of what is valuable, much as the Fool or Prophet might challenge.

You might wonder as you near the end of this book, what is your purpose? Maybe you were hoping the archetypes would illumine this. The invitation from the Monk is to consider, what if your purpose is simply paying attention and bringing reverence wherever you go? Contemplation invites us into a paradox in that it does not have a purpose or end goal but is always bringing us into deeper intimacy with the One who is already with us, already offering us generous grace in each moment, supporting us in imagining a renewed world.

In the stories of the Desert Fathers and Mothers, "Abba Sisoes said to a brother, 'How are you getting on?' and he replied: 'I am wasting my time, father.' The old man said, 'If I happen to waste a day, I am grateful for it.'"[6] The Monk treasures the gift of "wasting time" and yielding our agendas for the divine unfolding within each one of us.

Sabbath, which you were invited to inhabit in a previous chapter, is a taste of this. The purpose of practicing sabbath is to slowly see that the gift of rest and our value beyond what we do is available to us at all times. We can begin to inhabit the Paradise that is ours if only we pause and look.

MEDITATION: INVITING YOUR INNER MONK

Begin by finding your breath and deepening it slowly so that you savor the gift of air as it fills you and as you release it. Savor this rhythm of rising and falling, fullness and emptiness for a few breath cycles.

Allow your breath to draw your awareness down to your heart center. Be present to whatever your experience is right now, without trying to change it. Welcome any feelings that come, gently breathing. Rest into this place of connection to the source of infinite compassion. Lean into the divine grace sustaining you moment by moment, knowing there is nothing you need to do.

Welcome the presence of Thomas Merton; see how he wants to appear to you right now. Welcome the Spirit accompanying you on this inner journey. Ask Thomas and the Spirit to help reveal to you your inner Monk. Allow some time to be with this part of yourself and how she or he comes to you. What is the energy of this presence? Ask for wisdom and illumination of the way ahead and listen for the response.

Ask for a vision of the Paradise that is all around you already. Seek guidance for those times when you feel the anxiety and burdens of the world pressing down on you. What wisdom does the Monk have to offer you? Ask for the grace of one wise word. Is there a gift that can lighten the burden and remind you of the presence of this Paradise?

Rest into this experience for as long as you need to and then allow yourself to simply be in stillness for several moments, just

being in the moment guided by your breath and releasing all doing and striving.

Then slowly let your breath bring you back to the room and
record any insights you want to remember.

MANDALA EXPLORATION: CAIRNS

For our final experience, you are invited again to a contemplative
walk, this time somewhere you are likely to find stones, such as
along the shore of a river, a lake, or an ocean. You could also do
this exercise with landscaping stones if you don't have any good
locations nearby.

Begin with centering through your breath. Invite your inner
Monk to be with you in this experience, guiding your way. Ask
for what you need during this time of prayer. Release whatever
distractions are at hand.

As you walk, stay present to the stones and the ways they
might be calling to you. You will be gathering up several and creating a cairn, which is a vertical stack of stones. There are many
traditions that utilize cairns; in British Columbia, the Inuit First
Nations people build inukshuks, which are stone stacks meant as
markers of the way.

You might build a single one to place in the center of a large
open space, or you might build four, one for each of the four directions, creating a circle. You could also build five and combine
both of these together. Once you have completed the cairns, I
invite you to again walk the rounds around either the single cairn
in the center or the four cairns in the four directions.

Make this a prayerful walk in a sunwise direction. Let this be a
time of contemplating your own sacred center and the direction
of your life. How does the Monk help to illuminate your way?
Thomas Merton wrote in one of his poems,

the whole
world is secretly on fire, the stones
burn.[7]

You might want to receive this creation with a photo to record
it; check in and see how that feels. Thank the materials for their
invitation to participate with them in creating more beauty.

FOR REFLECTION

- What about Merton's story most inspires or energizes you?
  Where do you feel the strongest connection or disconnection?
- How is your inner Monk inviting you to be more present to
  your life?
- How might you practice paradise and discover the generosity of life here and now?
- What did the visual art exploration experience reveal to
  you?

CLOSING BLESSING

The poem that follows was inspired by the title question, which is
a quote from a poem written by Thomas Merton. I think Thomas
might appreciate the imagery. The call of the Monk is to allow
ourselves to drop into this silence, to drink from it regularly, and
to let it nourish us.

"Whose Silence Are You?"
After Thomas Merton
> The single eye of the sun long shut,
> world deep asleep like a sunken ship loaded with treasures,
> full moon's fierce shadows illumine the way for miles,
> stars glint like coins dropped to the well's black bottom,
> last apple fallen from the tree
> in a slush of honey and crimson.

I walk barefoot across wet grass,
night's questions relentlessly wrestling
in my mind's knotted weave.
I look for answers written by salmon in the stream,
or a snail's slither of streaming silver.
I prostrate myself at the gnarled foot of the ash tree.

River softly murmurs her secrets.
Then the wind departs, taking words with it.
Hush cracks open, and
only Silence
blankets my moss-covered dreams
under the mute howl of night.

The long slow leaving of voices reveals
the ancient song of repose.
I awaken covered with dew,
stillness shaken by a single robin.
No longer full of my own echoing emptiness,
I am able to hear at last.

May you feel the knot of questions in your mind untangle and slip away. May you discover what silence wants to whisper to you. And as we depart company together for now, may you remember this community of kindred souls as a source of solace in the days to come. May you remember the inner community inviting you into the great and cosmic dance.

Conclusion

. . . .

We have come to the end of this journey, which is really just a beginning. The invitation is to continue inviting in these energies and follow where they take you. There are other archetypes to explore; two favorites of mine not covered in this book are the Lover and the Magician. Look in the additional resources on pages 197–198 to find further reading material to introduce you to these and others.

My deepest hope is that by befriending some of these parts of yourself and welcoming them in, your way ahead has been illuminated a little bit more. Continue to invite this inner cast of characters into dialogue with you and with one another. When you are trying to make a decision, ask each one for their perspective and what they might have to offer in terms of wisdom.

This is a journey toward growing wholeness, where the fragments of ourselves are brought back together again.

Appendix: How to Practice Lectio Divina

Excerpted from *Lectio Divina—The Sacred Art: Transforming Words and Images into Heart-Centered Prayer* (SkyLight Paths Publishing) by Christine Valters Paintner.

FIRST MOVEMENT—*LECTIO*:
SETTLING AND SHIMMERING

Begin by finding a comfortable position where you can remain alert and yet also relax your body. Bring your attention to your breath and allow a few moments to become centered. If you find yourself distracted at any time, gently return to the rhythm of your breath as an anchor for your awareness. Allow yourself to settle into this moment and become fully present.

Read your selected scripture passage or other sacred text once or twice through slowly and listen for a word or phrase that feels significant right now and is capturing your attention even if you don't know why. Gently repeat this word to yourself in the silence.

SECOND MOVEMENT—*MEDITATIO*:
SAVORING AND STIRRING

Read the text again and then allow the word or phrase that caught your attention in the first movement to spark your imagination.

Savor the word or phrase with all of your senses; notice what smells, sounds, tastes, sights, and feelings are evoked. Then listen for what images, feelings, and memories are stirring, welcoming them in, and then savoring and resting into this experience.

THIRD MOVEMENT—*ORATIO*:
SUMMONING AND SERVING

Read the text a third time and then listen for an invitation rising up from your experience of prayer so far. Consider the word or phrase and what it has evoked for you in memory, image, or feeling; what is the invitation? This invitation may be a summons toward a new awareness or action.

FOURTH MOVEMENT—*CONTEMPLATIO*:
SLOWING AND STILLING

Move into a time for simply resting in God and allowing your heart to fill with gratitude for God's presence in this time of prayer. Slow your thoughts and reflections even further and sink into the experience of stillness. Rest in the presence of God and allow yourself to simply be. Rest here for several minutes. Return to your breath if you find yourself distracted.

CLOSING

Gently connect with your breath again and slowly bring your awareness back to the room, moving from inner experience to outer experience. Give yourself some time of transition between these moments of contemplative depth and your everyday life. Consider taking a few minutes to journal about what you experienced in your prayer.

ℕotes

· ·

INTRODUCTION

1. Walter Wink, "Easter: What Happened to Jesus?" *The Network of Spiritual Progressives*, accessed May 20, 2015, http://spiritualprogressives.org/newsite/?p=685.

2. Carl Jung, *The Collected Works of C. G. Jung*, ed. and trans. Gerhard Adler and R. F. C. Hull, vol. 11, *Psychology and Religion: West and East* (Princeton, NJ: Princeton University Press, 1969), 89.

3. Carl Jung, *Memories, Dreams, Reflections* (New York: Random House, 1961), 196–197.

4. DOROTHY DAY: THE ORPHAN

1. I first learned this fairy tale form from Orla McGovern in an improvisation class she teaches in Galway, Ireland.

5. AMMA SYNCLETICA: THE WARRIOR

1. *The Sayings of the Desert Fathers*, trans. by Benedicta Ward (Kalamazoo, MI: Cistercian Publications, 1975), 230–231.

2. Alan Jones, *Soul Making: The Desert Way of Spirituality* (San Francisco: Harper-Collins, 1989), 104.

3. Anthony J. Schulte, "Naming the 'Father Hunger': An Interview with Richard Rohr," *M.A.L.Es Web Site*, October 1990, http://www.stjamesstratford.com /files/Men's%20ministry%20documents/Father-Hunger[1].pdf.

6. BRIGID OF KILDARE: THE HEALER

1. Jan Richardson, "Feast of the Presentation/Candlemas" *The Painted Prayerbook*, February 2, 2008, http://paintedprayerbook.com/2008/02/02/feast-of-the-presentationcandlemas.

7. BRENDAN THE NAVIGATOR: THE PILGRIM

1. Cynthia Bourgeault, *Mystical Hope: Trusting in the Mercy of God* (Cambridge, MA: Cowley, 2001), 56–57.

2. Ibid., 18.

3. Ibid., 89.

4. Phil Cousineau, *The Art of Pilgrimage: The Seeker's Guide to Making Travel Sacred* (Berkeley, CA: Conari Press, 1998), xxvii.

9. MIRIAM: THE PROPHET

1. Walter Brueggemann, *Sabbath as Resistance: Saying No to the Culture of Now* (Louisville: Westminster John Knox Press, 2014).

2. Ibid., 5.

3. Scott Wright, *Oscar Romero and the Communion of Saints: A Biography* (Maryknoll, NY: Orbis Books, 2009), 153–154.

10. RAINER MARIA RIKE: THE ARTIST

1. Rainer Maria Rilke, *Letters to a Young Poet* (Novato, CA: New World Library, 2000), 11.

2. Ibid., 80.

3. Rainer Maria Rilke, *Rilke: Selected Letters*, ed. Harry T. Moore (New York: Anchor Books, 1960), 193.

4. Rainer Maria Rilke, *Rilke's Book of Hours: Love Poems to God*, trans. Anita Barrows and Joanna Macy (New York: Riverhead Books, 1996), 58.

5. Rainer Maria Rilke, *Selected Poems of Rainer Maria Rilke*, trans. Robert Bly (New York: Harper and Row, 1981), 27.

6. Rainer Maria Rilke, *The Poet's Guide to Life: The Wisdom of Rilke* (New York: Random House, 2005), 141.

7. *The Sayings of the Desert Fathers*, 179, 224.

8. John Fox, *Finding What You Didn't Lose: Expressing Your Truth and Creativity through Poem-Making* (New York: Tarcher Books, 1995), 78–80.

11. HILDEGARD OF BINGEN: THE VISIONARY

1. *Symphony of the Harmony of Celestial Revelations*, trans. Barbara Newman (Cornell, NY: Cornell University Press, 1988), 141.

12. THOMAS MERTON: THE MONK

1. Thomas Merton, *New Seeds of Contemplation* (New York: New Directions, 2007), 296–297.

2. Thomas Merton, *The Waters of Siloe* (New York: Harcourt Brace, 1949), 274.

3. Thomas Merton, *Thoughts in Solitude* (New York: Farrar, Straus and Giroux, 1999), 92.

4. Thomas Merton, *Conjectures of a Guilty Bystander* (New York: Doubleday Image, 1968), 81.

5. Douglas E. Christie, *Blue Sapphire of the Mind: Notes for a Contemplative Ecology* (New York: Oxford University Press, 2012), 314.

6. *The Sayings of the Desert Fathers*, 222.

7. Thomas Merton, *Collected Poems of Thomas Merton* (New York: New Directions, 1977), 281.

Additional Resources

MULTIMEDIA RESOURCES

Singing with Monks and Mystics. Twelve songs inspired by each of the monks and mystics featured in this book. Order at AbbeyoftheArts.com.

Dancing with Monks and Mystics. Twelve dance prayers choreographed by Betsey Beckman. Order at AbbeyoftheArts.com.

Full-color prints of the dancing monk icons included in this book are available at AbbeyoftheArts.com.

To see more of Marcy Hall's artwork, visit her online at RabbitRoomArts.blogspot.com.

To see more artwork by Stacy Wills, who created the mandala coloring pages, visit her online at StacyWills.com.

THE ARCHETYPES

Edinger, Edward. *Ego and Archetype.* Boston: Shambhala Publications, 1992.

Hunter, Allan, L. *The Six Archetypes of Love: From Innocent to Magician.* London: Findhorn Press, 2008.

Jung, C. G. *Collected Works of C. G. Jung, Volume 9 (Part 1): Archetypes and the Collective Unconscious.* Princeton, NJ: Princeton University Press, 1981.

Moore, Robert. *King, Warrior, Magician, Lover: Rediscovering the Archetypes of the Mature Masculine.* San Francisco: HarperOne, 2013.

Myss, Caroline. *Archetypes.* Carlsbad, CA: Hay House, 2013.

Pearson, Carol. *Awakening the Heroes Within: Twelve Archetypes to Help Us Find Ourselves and Transform Our World.* New York: HarperCollins, 2012.

Wauters, Ambika. *Chakras and Their Archetypes: Uniting Energy Awareness and Spiritual Growth.* Berkeley, CA: Crossing Press, 1997.

MONKS AND MYSTICS

Day, Dorothy. *The Duty of Delight: The Diaries of Dorothy Day*. Abridged edition. New York: Image, 2011.

de Waal, Esther. *Seeking God: The Way of St. Benedict*. Collegeville, MN: Liturgical Press, 2001.

Dowrick, Stephanie. *In the Company of Rilke: Why a 20th-Century Visionary Poet Speaks So Eloquently to 21st-Century Readers*. New York: Tarcher Books, 2011.

Gafney, Wilda. *Daughters of Miriam: Women Prophets in Ancient Israel*. Philadelphia: Fortress Press, 2008.

Merton, Thomas. *New Seeds of Contemplation*. New York: New Directions, 2007.

Newman, Barbara. *Voice of the Living Light: Hildegard of Bingen and Her World*. Berkeley, CA: University of California Press, 1998.

O'Meara, John J. *Voyage of St Brendan*. Dublin: Dolmen Press, 1981.

Pinsky, Robert. *The Life of David*. New York: Schocken, 2005.

Richo, David. *Mary Within Us: A Jungian Contemplation of Her Titles and Powers*. Berkeley, CA: Human Development Books, 2013.

Rohr, Richard. *Eager to Love: The Alternative Way of Francis of Assisi*. Cincinnati: Franciscan Media, 2014.

Swan, Laura. *The Forgotten Desert Mothers: Sayings, Lives, and Stories of Early Christian Women*. Mahwah, NJ: Paulist Press, 2001.

Wright, Brian. *Brigid: Goddess, Druidess and Saint*. Mount Pleasant, SC: The History Press, 2009.

Christine Valters Paintner is the online abbess for Abbey of the Arts, a virtual monastery offering classes and resources on contemplative practice and creative expression. She earned a doctorate in Christian spirituality from the Graduate Theological Union in Berkeley, California, and achieved professional status as a registered expressive arts consultant and educator from the International Expressive Arts Therapy Association.

Paintner is the author of nine books on monasticism and creativity, including *Eyes of the Heart*; *Water, Wind, Earth, and Fire*; *The Artist's Rule*; and *The Soul of a Pilgrim*. She is a columnist for the progressive Christian portal at Patheos. She leads pilgrimages in Ireland, Austria, and Germany and online retreats at her website, abbeyofthearts.com, living out her commitment as a Benedictine Oblate in Galway, Ireland, with her husband, John.

Find more books by
Christine Valters
Paintner

wherever books and eBooks are sold.
For more information, **visit avemariapress.com.**